Recrudescence

in Memory of
Jean Salvato

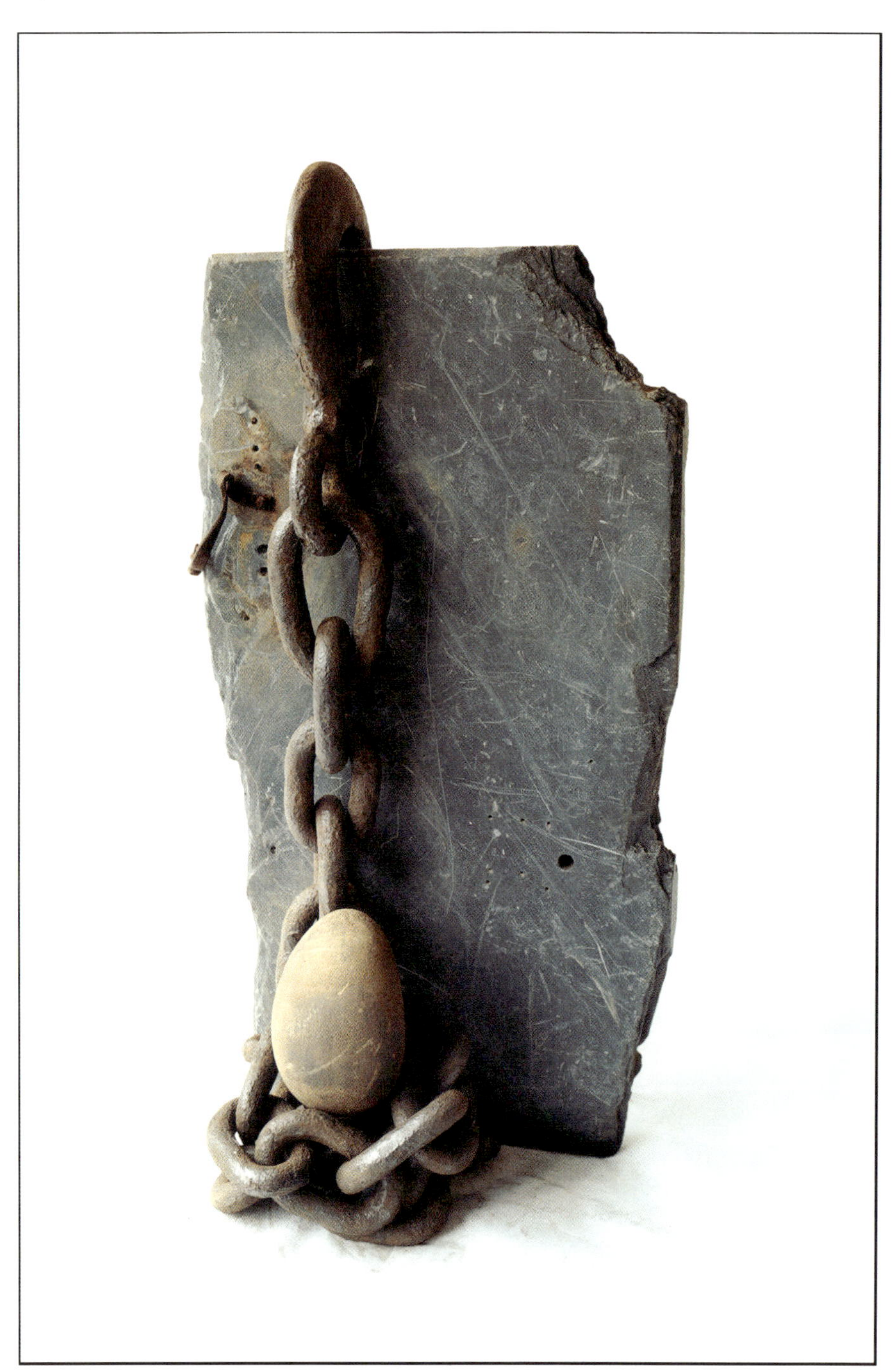

Recrudescence

a collaboration by

Michael Picarsic III and Lorraine Vullo

Introduction by Donald Kuspit

with an essay by Graham Shearing

Rivers of Steel National Heritage Area, Publisher

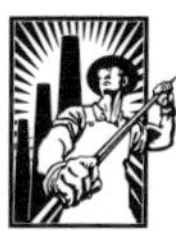

recrudescence

re • cru • des • cence *n.* the state of breaking out into renewed activity after an inactive or dormant period; the condition of renewal, or of returning to a raw or primary state. *(From the Latin* recrudescere, *"to grow raw again.")*

Copyright © 2005 by Michael Picarsic III and Lorraine Vullo

All rights reserved. No part of the contents of this book may be reproduced without the prior written permission of Michael Picarsic III and/or Lorraine Vullo.

Published in the United States by Rivers of Steel National Heritage Area.
Printed in the United States by J.B. Kreider Printing Company, Inc.

ISBN 0-9754462-1-5

Library of Congress Control Number: 2005926917

First Edition.

This book is printed on acid-free paper.

Excerpts from "Two Chorale-Preludes" and "The Songbook of Sebastian Arrurruz" from *NEW AND COLLECTED POEMS, 1952–1992* by Geoffrey Hill. Copyright © 1994 by Geoffrey Hill. Reprinted by permission of Houghton Mifflin Company. All rights reserved.

Front cover—Construction XXXIX, 2003. 5 x 4 inches
Frontispiece—Prometheus, 2004. Slate, rusting steel and stone, 32.75 x 17.75 x 14 inches
Back cover—Eros, 2003. Stone and brick, 9.5 x 5 x 5 inches

Contents

Introduction Donald Kuspit

Memorializing and Mythologizing Big Steel:
The Picarsic/Vullo Recrudescence Project

7

Essay Graham Shearing

Recrudescence: The Project

11

Constructions

17

Structures

45

A Note from August R. Carlino

73

Acknowledgments

74

Introduction

Memorializing and Mythologizing Big Steel: The Picarsic/Vullo
Recrudescence Project

It's the profoundest idea of art: making the past good–
memorializing and mythologizing it– by turning it into art. Art
is reparative, the psychoanalyst Melanie Klein famously argued,
and seduces us to life when there is no reason to believe in it, as
the philosopher Friedrich Nietzsche asserted. In other words, art
effects an emotional revolution, a "transvaluation of values"– the
transformation of the negative into the positive, the ugly real
into the eloquent ideal, the traumatic into the transcendental– as
Nietzsche said. The term "recrudescence" epitomizes this idea:
it means "breaking out afresh or into renewed activity, revival or
reappearance into active existence," as the dictionary says. Michael
Picarsic's and Lorraine Vullo's Recrudescence Project literally
embodies the idea: they restore the inert materials of a dead world
to active life by recycling them in fresh art– aesthetically convincing
and emotionally moving art, which is what the photographs and
sculptures that constitute the project are.

The Recrudescence Project is redemptive: it symbolizes and
celebrates the power of Big Steel– once the glory of Pittsburgh–
even as it mourns its passing. Picarsic and Vullo rescue relics of
it from the funeral pyre of the past and elevate them into subtly
sublime art without erasing the scars of time that mark them.
Rusted, broken *memento mori* become enigmatic art. It is an act
of homage to Big Steel, ironically reduced to a shadow of itself
in small works of art– certainly small compared to the factories
in which steel was produced. Scavenged, impersonal scraps
become intimate abstract sculptures– a triumph of creativity over
destruction: good can come from bad. And then, as though to
express nostalgia for what has been, as well as to document what
they acknowledge is ephemeral– as ephemeral as Pittsburgh's steel

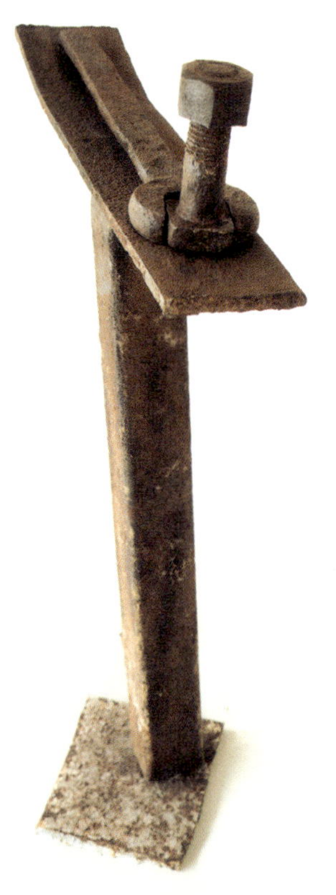

Hephaestus, 2005
Rusting steel, 30 x 10 x 19 inches

industry, once so vigorous everyone thought it would last forever– Picarsic and Vullo photograph the sculptures with four pinhole cameras. It is the most primitive kind of camera. They built the cameras themselves out of discarded found materials, like those used to build their sculptures. There is an ingenious conceptual symmetry between camera and sculpture, especially because both are ironical constructions.

Just as the sculptures rescued waste material from the site before it would be dumped into oblivion, so the photographs rescue the sculptures from the site before they could be destroyed by its redevelopment. Noticing that their "building materials were being ground up, buried, or hauled out," they removed "the most aesthetically pleasing scraps from the site and rebuil[t] them into smaller sculptures"– these became the series they call Structures. The site is all-important: "an enormous piece of land," as Picarsic and Vullo say, that was once the location of a Jones & Laughlin steel mill. In operation from the 1900s through the 1960s, it was razed in 1989. "We wandered around and found a lifeless landscape decorated with rusted steel, railroad ties, smashed sheet metal, river rocks, broken glass, huge concrete slabs, hillsides covered with bricks, and a plethora of other odd and interesting pieces that had use when the steel industry flourished." They used these fragments to create sculptures, "some very simple and spontaneous," others that "took the entire day to build," physically exhausting them. Clearly Picarsic and Vullo identify with the workers who once made steel in the mill, an activity they implicitly regard as creative. They clearly regard all work– like the forgotten steel workers, they work with their hands as well as minds– as arduous and creative. Certainly their hard, persistent work is a tribute to the steel workers. Their relentless activity in and of itself is emblematic of the ambition that was once Big Steel.

Turning raw ruins into refined art is a seemingly magical alchemical process, like the conversion of crude iron ore fresh from the earth into finished hard steel serving the purposes of civilization. Indeed, the alchemical ambition of transforming dark, meaningless *prima materia* into luminous, meaningful *ultima materia* led directly to the development of the sophisticated chemistry involved in making steel. I suggest that the transformation of *prima materia* into *ultima materia* is more complete in the Structures than in the Constructions by reason of their titles. The Constructions are anonymous assemblages of raw material, while the Structures are larger-than-life mythological personages. The titles are an alchemical supplement that gives the sculptures an unexpected depth of meaning. The Structures are about the revival and reappearance– to recall the definition of "recrudescence"– of the ancient gods as well as the steel industry. In antiquity they took naturalistic form, which is alchemized into abstract form in modernity. Both forms are artistic, but the latter is openly spiritual compared to the former.

I am suggesting that the Structures are spiritual, not simply physical, objects. Their grand inner scale suggests as much. They remind us of the enduring hold Greek mythology exerts on our imagination, and suggest that the ancient gods continue to live within us. Certainly Hephaestus– the Greek god of fire, metal-working, and handicrafts, and the model for the alchemist– was the reigning god of Pittsburgh in the heyday of the steel industry. He continues to haunt it. *Hephaestus*, 2005 seems emblematic of the entire Recrudescence Project. It shows that Picarsic and Vullo understand the inner spirit of Pittsburgh, clearly a mythological and heroic place when steel ruled it.

Donald Kuspit
New York
May 2005

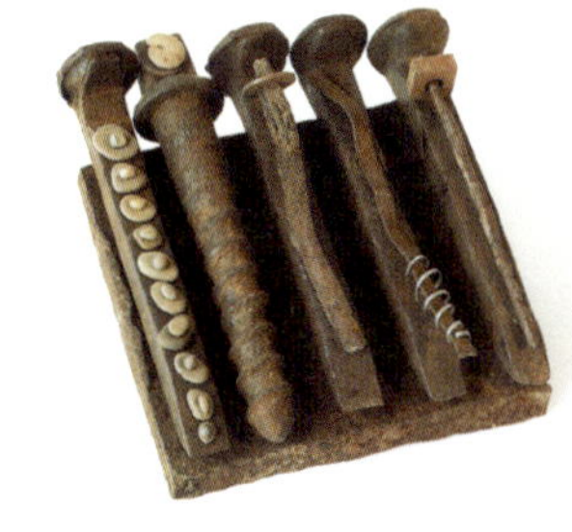

Five Rivers Surrounding the Underworld, 2005
Rusting steel and stone, 2 x 6.5 x 7 inches

Recrudescence: The Project

There is a land called Lost
At peace inside our heads.
The moon, full on the frost,
Vivifies these stone heads.

Moods of the verb 'to stare',
Split selfhoods, conjugate
Ice facets from the air,
the light glazing the light.

Look at us, Queen of Heaven.
Our solitudes drift by
your solitudes, the seven
dead stars in your sky.

Geoffrey Hill
Tenebrae, 1978, from *Two Chorale-Preludes*

A piece of driftwood, picked up on a seashore, a stone, washed by countless tides, a fragment of broken glass, worn down by the sand and a rusty shard of iron, are all emotive trifles. They have fuelled the imaginations of artists and poets over time and have often been transformed into profound works of art. It is perhaps less common for an industrial wasteland to yield up such things, and rarer still for this debris to be so profoundly considered. The industrial archaeologist has a different way with it, more analytical and more structured. Michael Picarsic and Lorraine Vullo crept into such a field, without a claim of right, as interlopers, to value their findings quite differently, with original eyes.

It is reasonable enough to extract from their work a special elegy for the vanished steel industry of Pittsburgh, for the site of their labor was one of the greatest steel mills in the world, a 'satanic' mill in the eyes of some, implacably consuming both

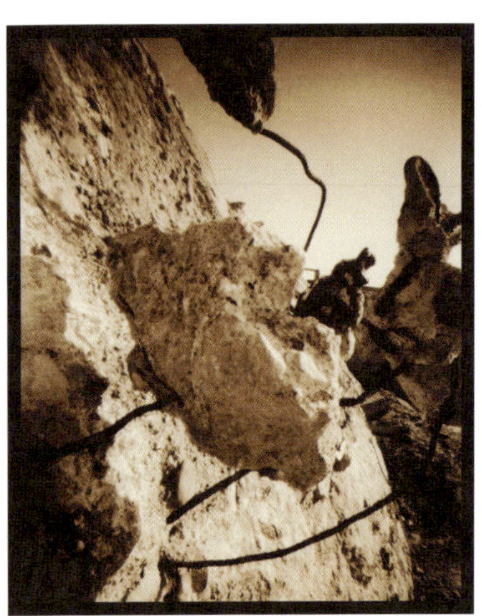

Construction X, 2003. 5 x 4 inches

men and materials alike. And creating with equal indifference the stuffing of both good and evil, ploughshares or swords. It is a true elegy, written in an urban graveyard, and made doubly elegiac for the graveyard itself is now gone too, and replaced by newer things, shopping malls and office buildings. The artists had to be quick, exploiting the narrowest window of opportunity.

Other artists had done similar things at about the same time in the region. Photographers who had documented the great buildings of industry have been moved to document the empty spaces left by them. Yet more artists had picked up large and small fragments and created large and small sculptures with them. Performance artists had intervened in the spaces too. It was as if the Spirit of Steel had willed it itself. But in the two years that Picarsic and Vullo had to themselves a greater engagement may be perceived.

Creeping, most definitely uninvited, onto this private property, slyly avoiding security men, sometimes inveigling them into some occasional complicity ("We are harmless artists, and possibly mad"–) they colonized this barren, near lunar, landscape. Rearranging (if 'rearranging' is the word for lugging hundred-pound blocks of concrete) the debris of broken bricks and bent iron girders into sculptural constructions, they built up temporary installations, which they proceeded to photograph. Such structures were highly vulnerable, since construction workers might at any moment dismantle, however unwittingly, the day's work.

These temporary installations, created in the rough terrain of a changing construction site, are to become the key works that subtly determine the pattern of the whole of the Recrudescence Project. Made *in situ,* of essential found objects, they are picked up, appraised and fitted together as *constructions.* They will be known as *Constructions* when later printed as a photographic series. But they have an ephemeral life as sculptural installations. They are like sandcastles built on the seashore, only to be washed away by the tide. They are known to us now only by the memorializing art of photography. Like Proust's *madeleine* they are gone, eaten up, and only recollected through photography. Photography is a step away from the real thing, distanced by intervening processes. Color and scale are subtracted from the reality, supplanted by sepia tones and the flatness of two-dimensional representation. What they lose they also gain.

A possible reading of these constructions and of the photographs that result is one of ruination. Ruins have always been perceived as site of contemplation, where the viewer can reflect on mortality and on the impermanence of things. The poet Ovid reminds us that now grasses grow where Troy once stood *(Iam seges est ubi troia fuit:* Ovid, *Heroides).*

Picarsic and Vullo are perhaps best known as photographers, and devised highly unusual methods of producing their images. (It is impossible to identify the voice of either one of them in this collaboration.) They created out of discarded and unwanted objects the tools of their trade. A filing cabinet became a pinhole camera, the most primitive of optical instruments. Discarded, out-of-date sheet film, even of the old X-ray variety, was employed. They made their own paper from discarded scraps of rag paper, and produced their own photographic chemicals and solutions that would not have disgraced a photographer from the nineteenth century. They bring to life dead things by dead methods.

To have slipped quietly away from their scenes of criminal trespass to the security of the developing room could have been enough, certainly sufficient to supply material for a decent exhibition and perhaps an illustrated book. The developing processes with their chancy technologies and processes have, in fact, continued to preoccupy them. Instead, they embarked upon a praiseworthy course of petty crime, removing bricks and scraps to a safe place and continuing to work on them as sculptures and installations. These, and their photographs, emerged in 2003 in an exhibition in Carnegie, a gritty township just outside of Pittsburgh, which might almost have been named for the art itself. (By coincidence, the vast sculpture by Richard Serra which stands at the door of the Carnegie Museum of Art in Pittsburgh is entitled *Carnegie.* It is made of Cor-Ten steel.) Other sculptural installations by them have found their ways into private gardens and houses in the region. All have been documented, by regular photography.

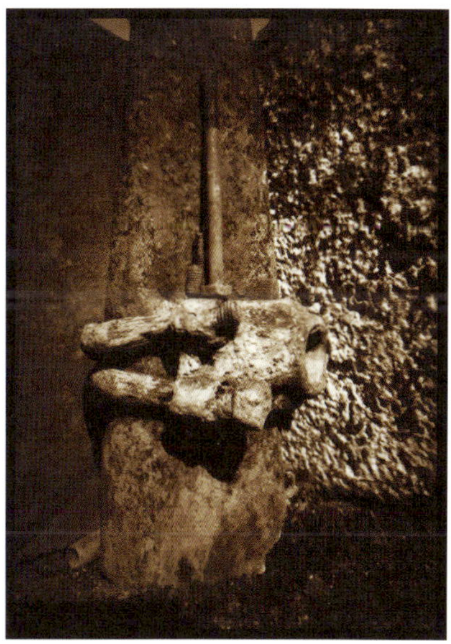

Construction LXIX, 2003. 7 x 5 inches

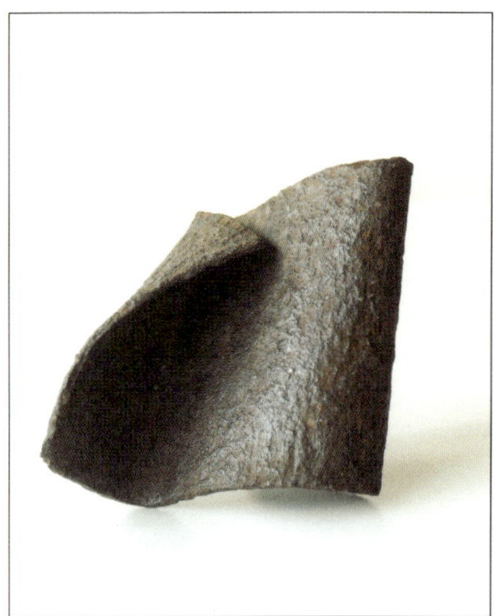

Morpheus, 2005
Rusting steel, 5.25 x 5 x 6.75 inches

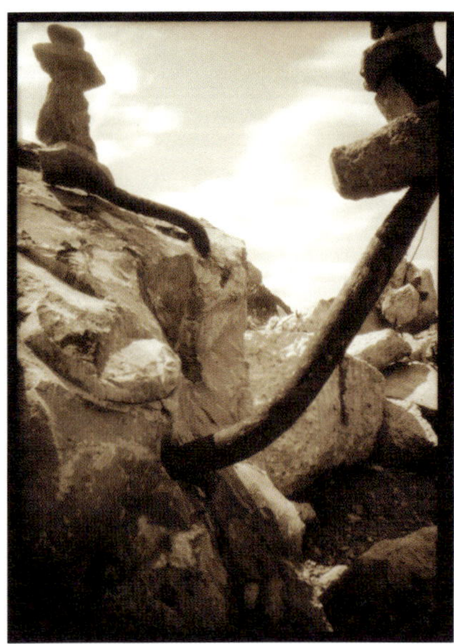

Construction XXXIV, 2003. 7 x 5 inches

The operation now shifts to a studio in Homestead, another site of Steel, and the locus of the notorious Homestead Strike of 1892. There Pinkerton's men, at Frick and Carnegie's behest, fired on the steelworkers, bringing to an end the strike, but indelibly embittering industrial relations in the nation. It is as if Picarsic and Vullo cannot avoid Steel.

But in that studio an important exercise in distancing takes place, not so much steel refining but rather as artistic refining. Here the sculptures sit, some already assembled, some awaiting assembly. On tables unused fragments are lined up with near scientific precision. They are being given names, extraordinary ones, for they are being baptized into the pantheon of classical mythology. To call one such piece (they are known collectively as *Structures) Hephaestus* may come as no surprise, he who was the smith and metal founder of the gods. Nor *Prometheus,* who stole fire from Hephaestus' forge to give it to man, countering Zeus's orders. That makes sense, but the naming of work after other gods or incidents in classical mythology indicates that the Structures now breathe a life of their own. They have cast off the mantle of their material and origin. So *Echo, Amphitrite, Poseidon, Morpheus* come into existence, with *Apollo's Arrow* and the *Five Rivers Surrounding the Underworld.* And I think that the artists are making a further claim for their work in that although constructed after the fashion of contemporary sculpture with found elements (as with Picasso, Moore and Duchamp), there is some connection with the entire history of sculpture.

At the rear of the studio is the darkroom. There too may be found an archaizing element. Nobody who sees these photographs is reminded of modern documentary trends. Although they are simple photographs, documenting what the pinhole aperture is aimed at, they are essentially unaltered and unedited. The methods and processes have greater associations with historic photography. Printed in black and white (some have been printed in Van Dyke browns), on matte surfaces as contact prints, they convey the aura of the past. And the finished compositions have no obvious sense of scale… a tiny print (as in *Construction XII)* can have a real sense of the monumental and *vice versa*. Taken out of context and without any sense of reference to Steel they become almost abstract.

Both Picarsic and Vullo in their other work have made a practice of decontextualising their subject matter. The decayed body of a turtle is nothing but a luxuriant composition of blacks and half shadow. The texture of skin is enlarged into a diffused and emotive tonality. In the case of each one there is a stepping back from reality to a private abstraction and to the play of formal concerns. That, of course, is where the artists take leave of any association with the past, with any history or any other concern, and makes them very much our contemporaries.

The poet Geoffrey Hill, whose eye falls on objects and memory with such devastating effect, offers a taut guide to the reading of Picarsic and Vullo:

> *'See how each fragment kindles as we turn it,*
> *At the end, into the light of appraisal'.*

Geoffrey Hill: King Log, 1968, *The Songbook of Sebastian Arrurruz, 4.*

Graham Shearing
Pittsburgh, PA
June 2005

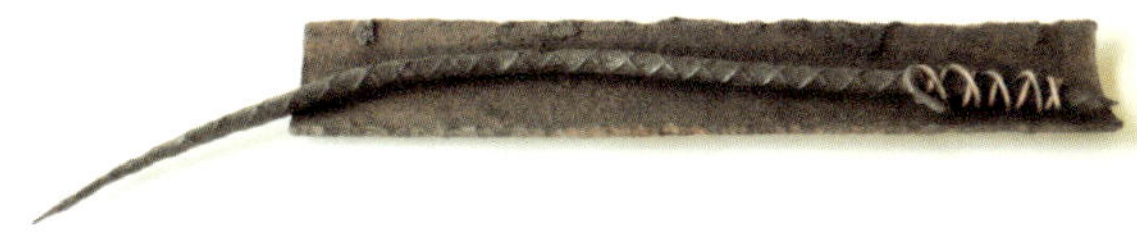

Apollo's Arrow, 2005
Rusting steel and copper wire, 1 x 16 x 4 inches

Constructions

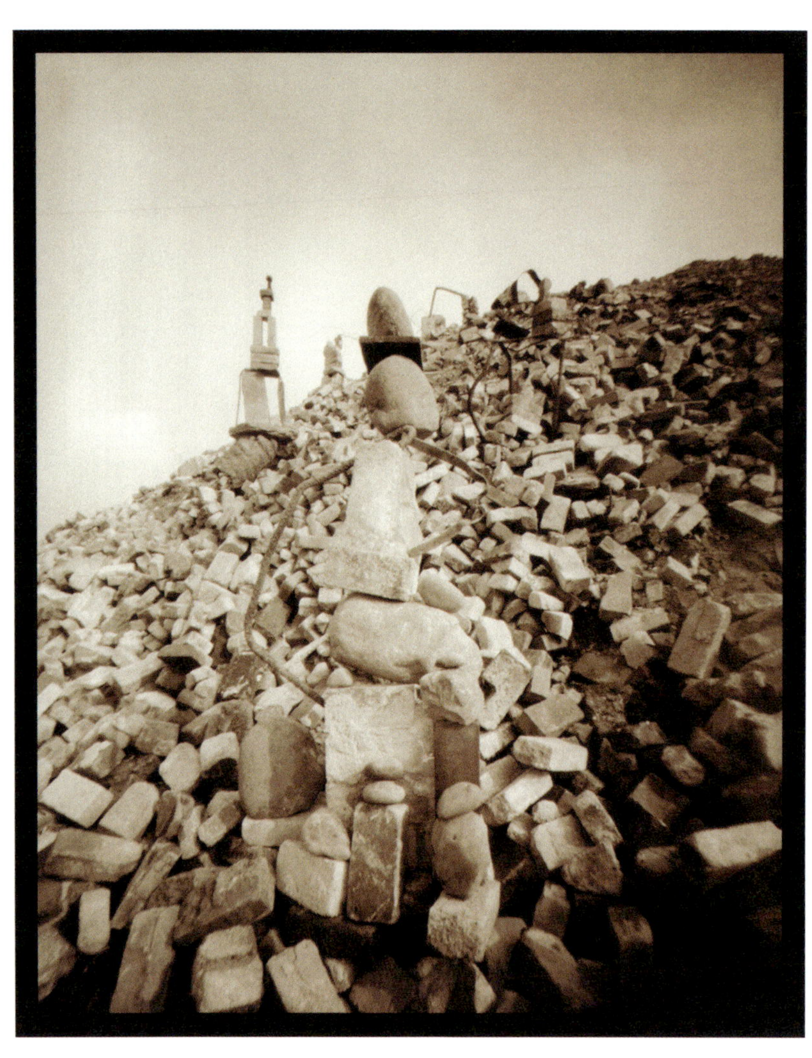

Construction XIX, 2003. 5 x 4 inches

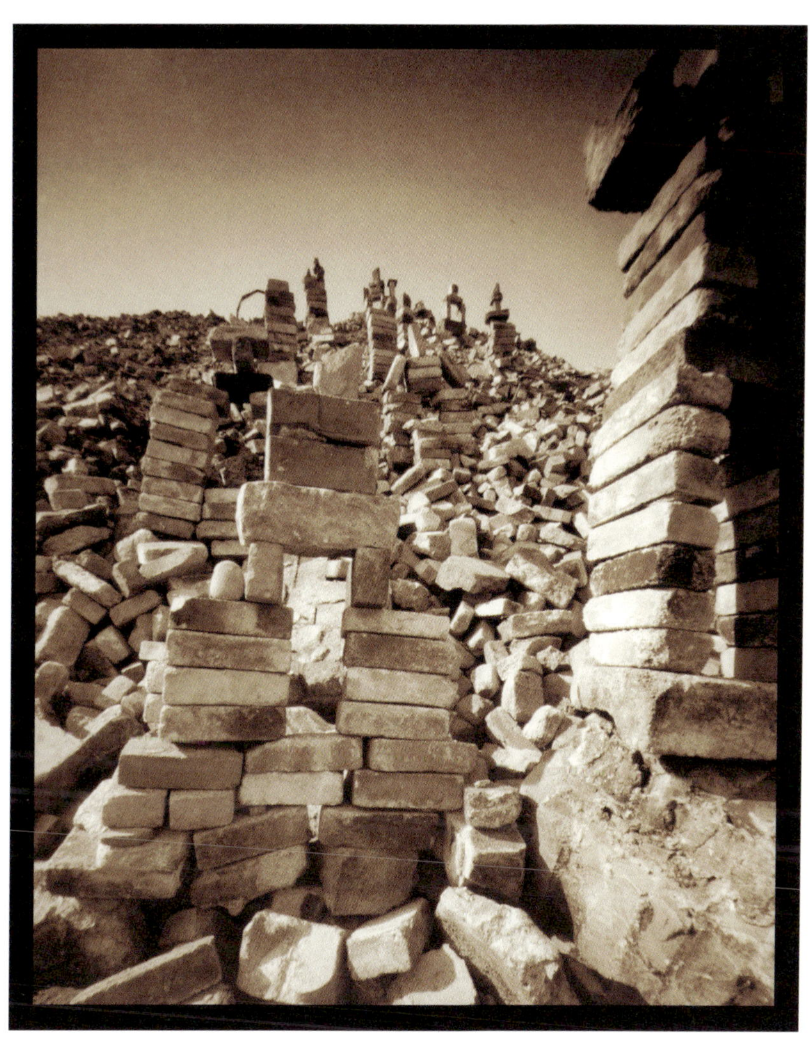

Construction XII, 2003. 5 x 4 inches

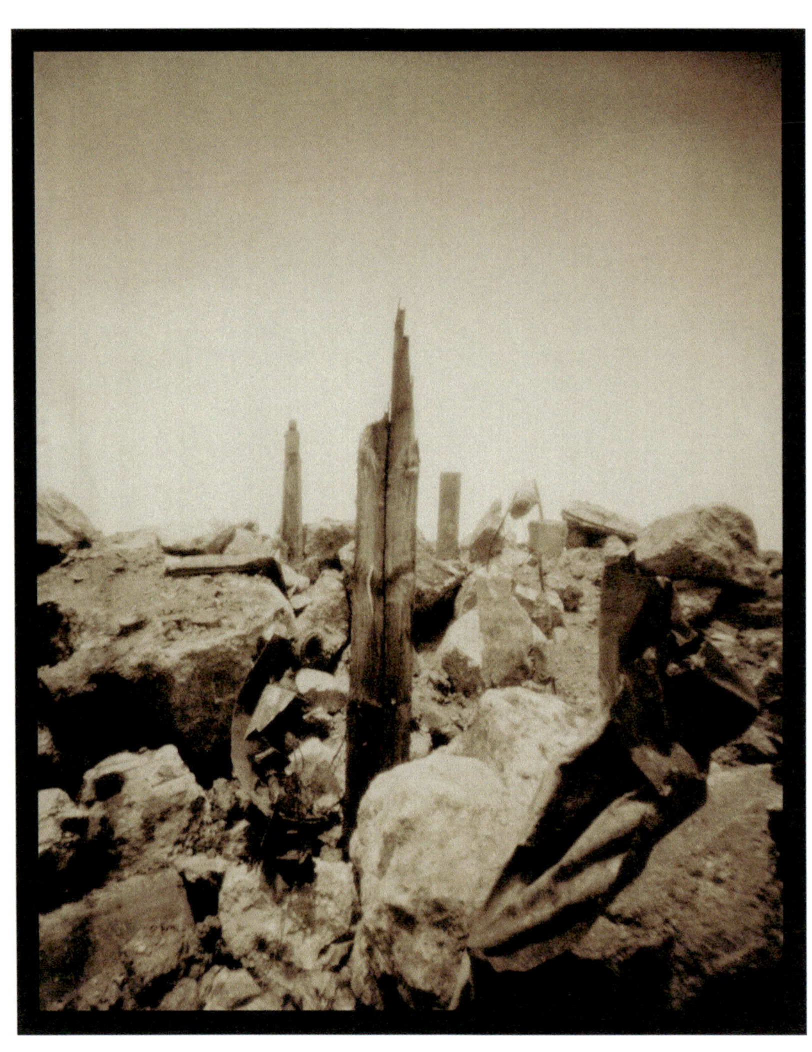

Construction I, 2003. 5 x 4 inches

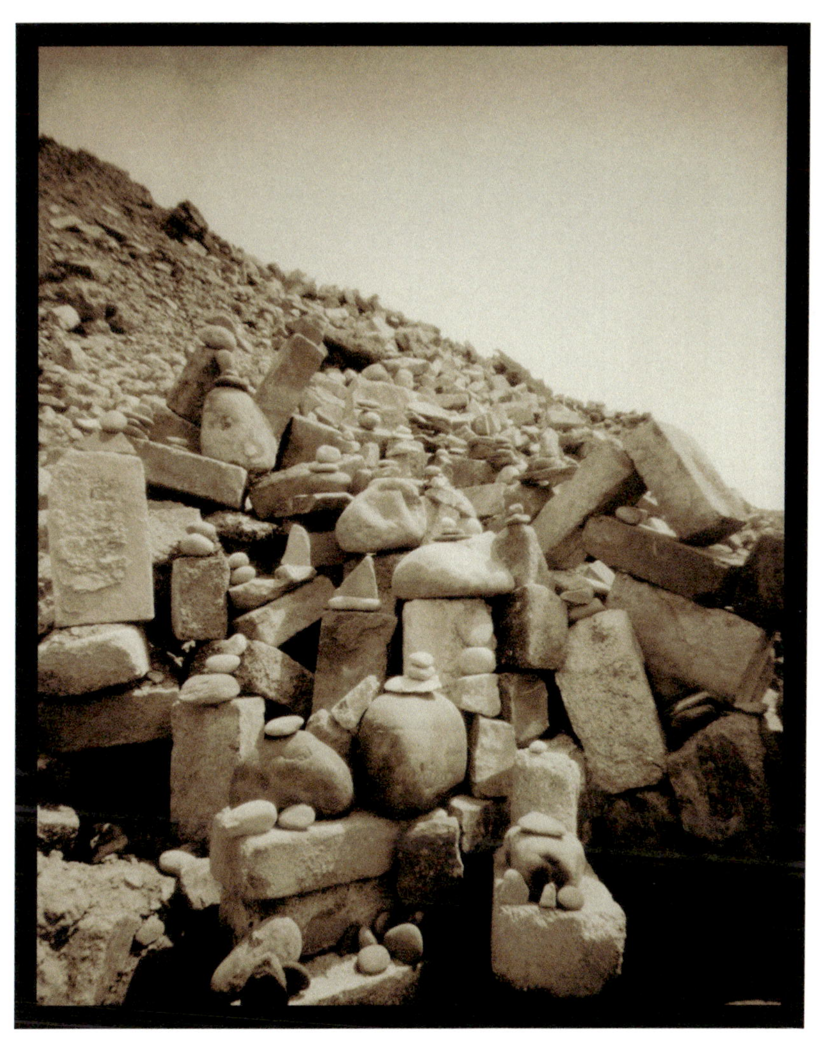

Construction IX, 2003. 5 x 4 inches

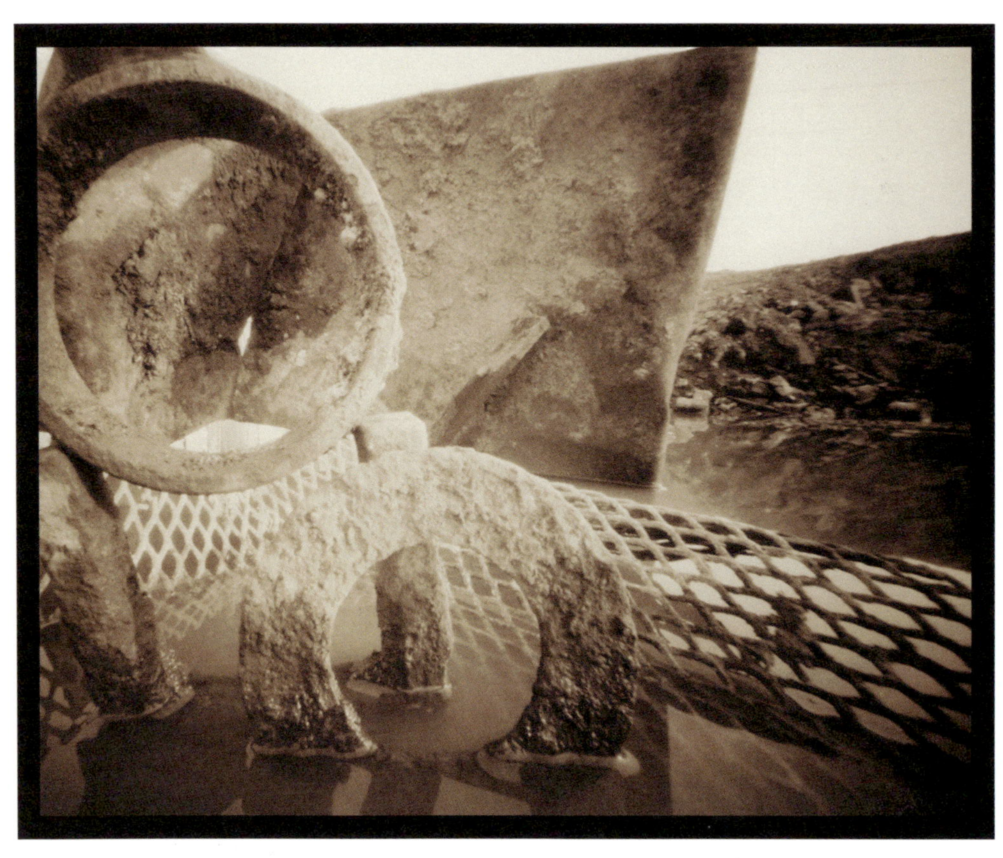

Construction LXV, 2003. 4 x 5 inches

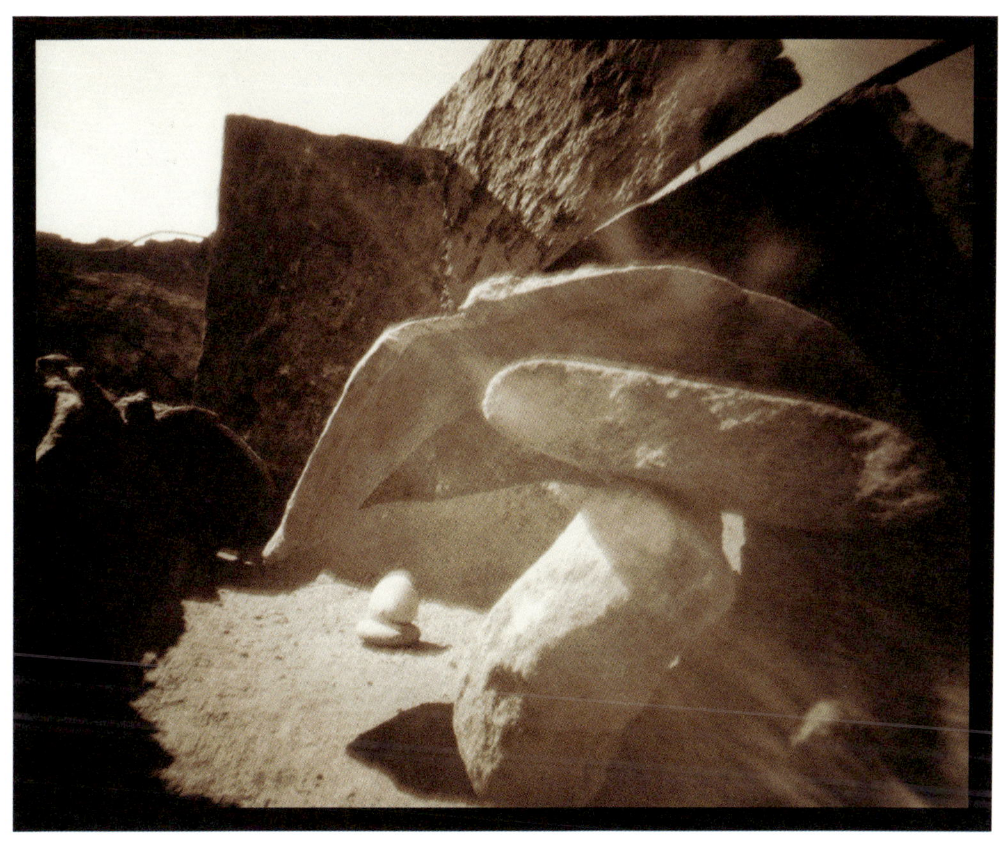

Construction LI, 2003. 4 x 5 inches

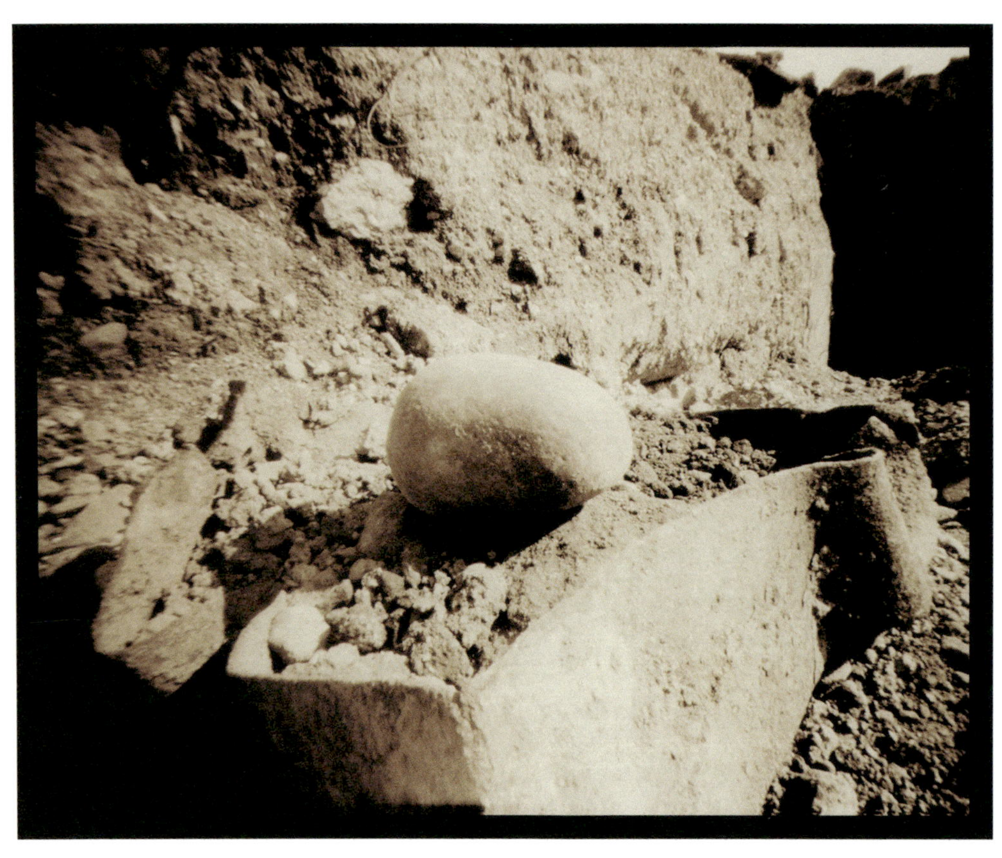

Construction VIII, 2003. 4 x 5 inches

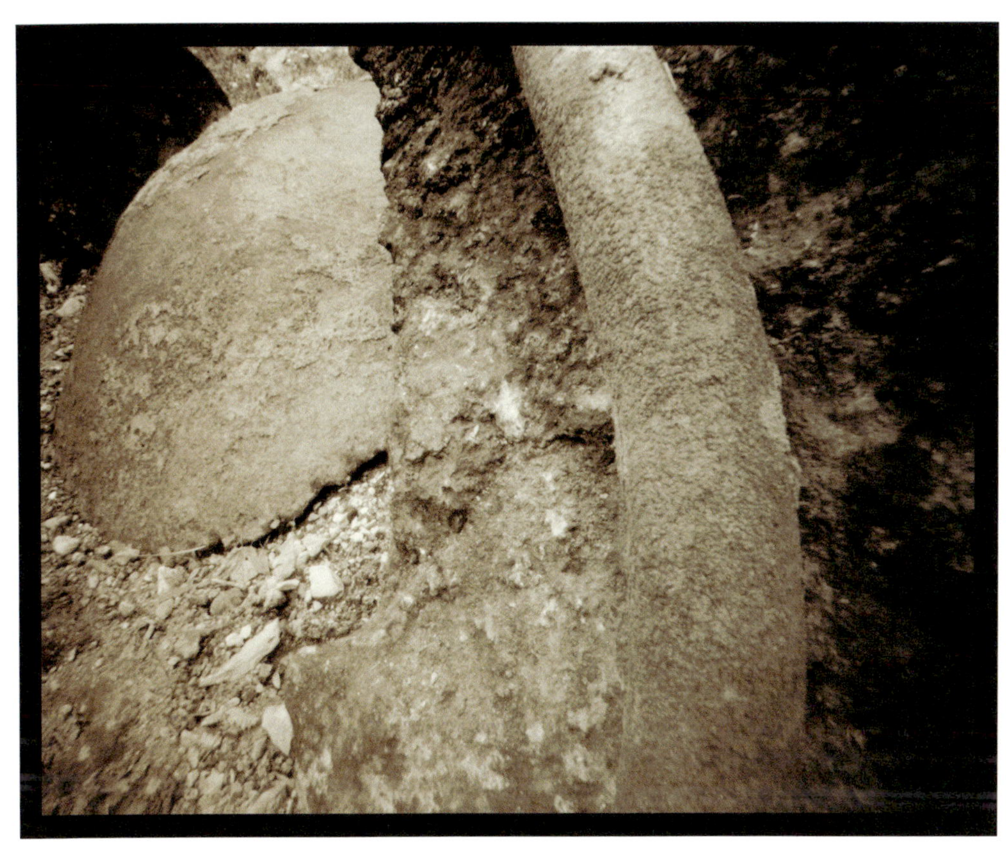

Construction II, 2003. 4 x 5 inches

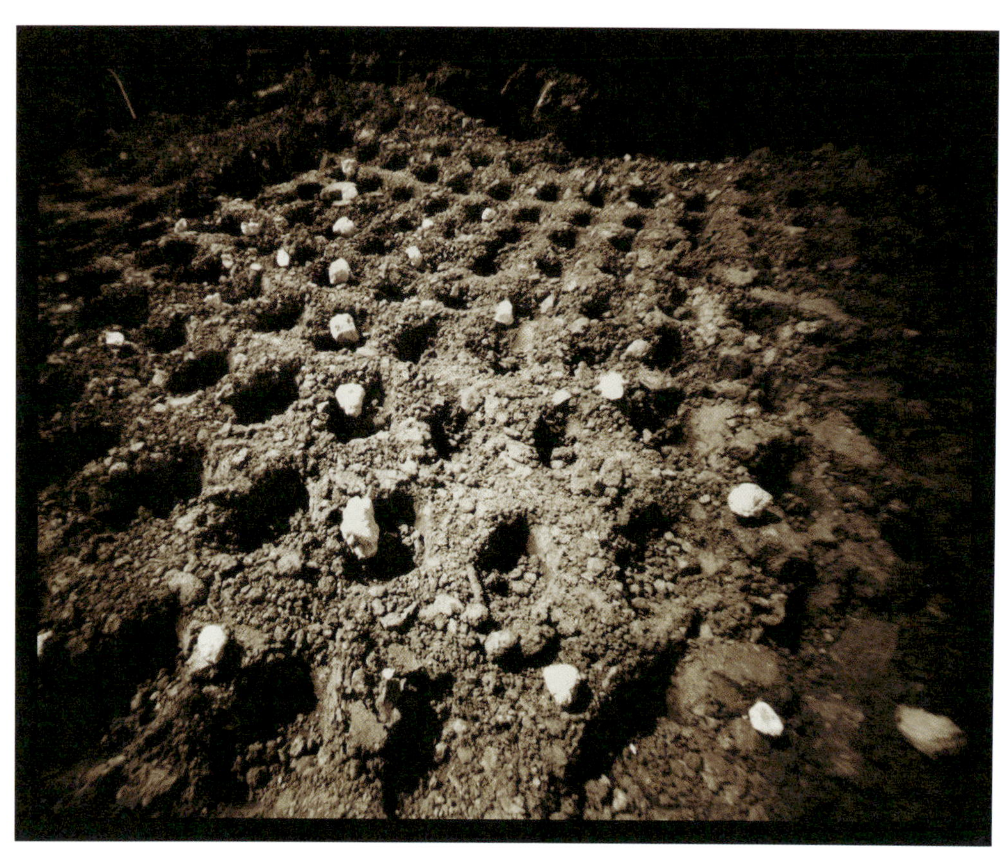

Construction XXXVIII, 2003. 4 x 5 inches

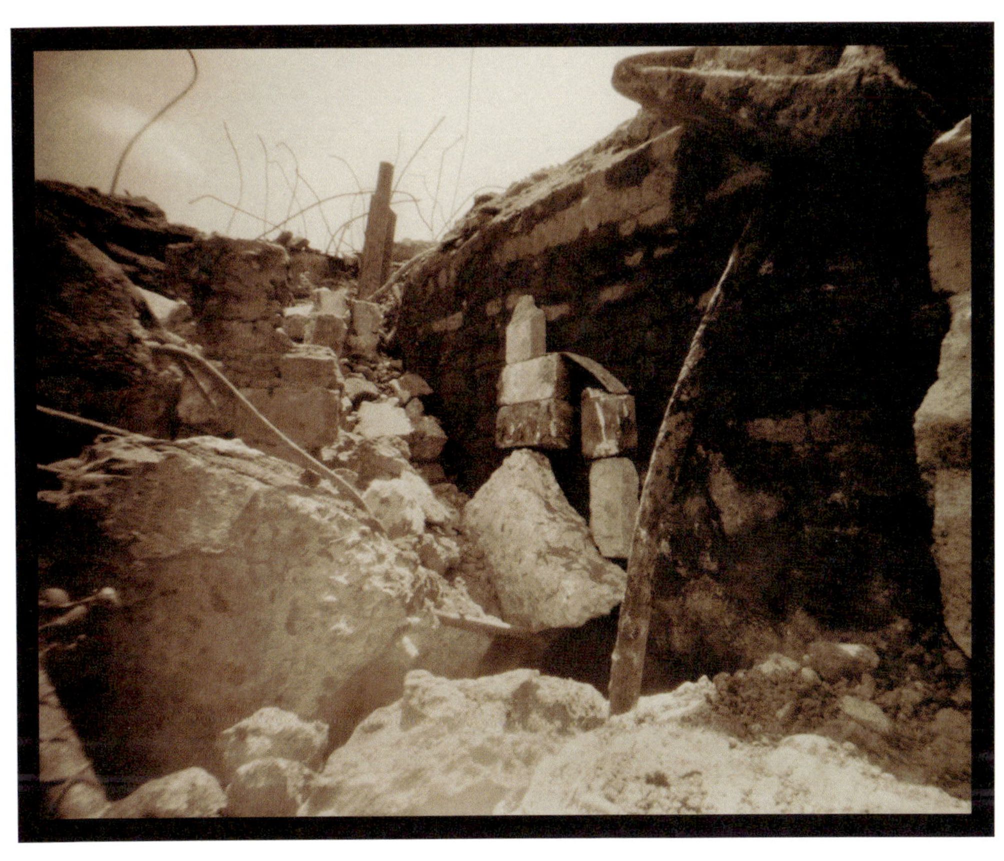

Construction XI, 2003. 4 x 5 inches

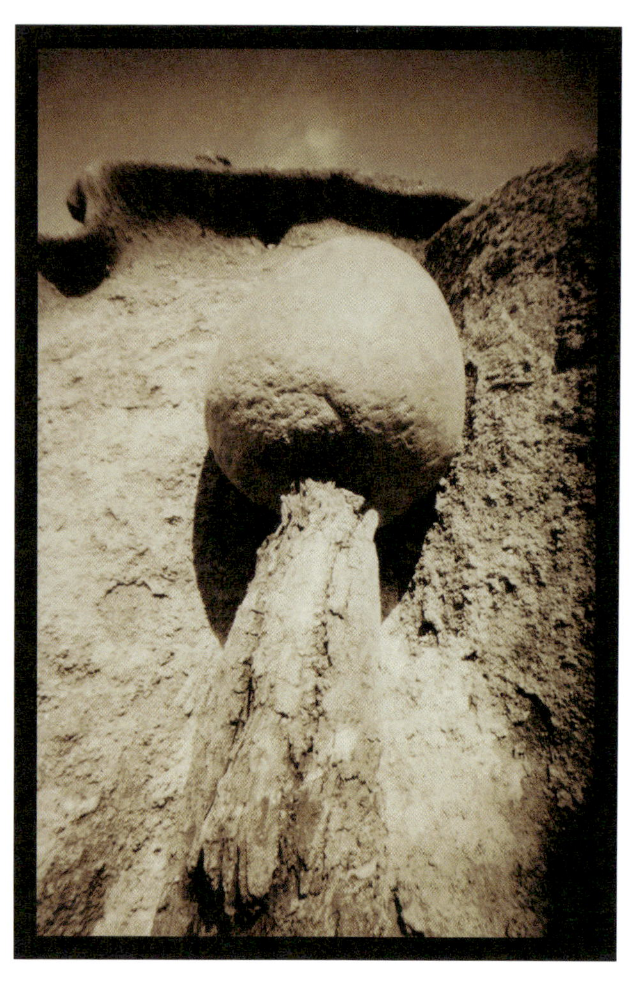

Construction VIIIa, 2003. 5.50 x 3 inches

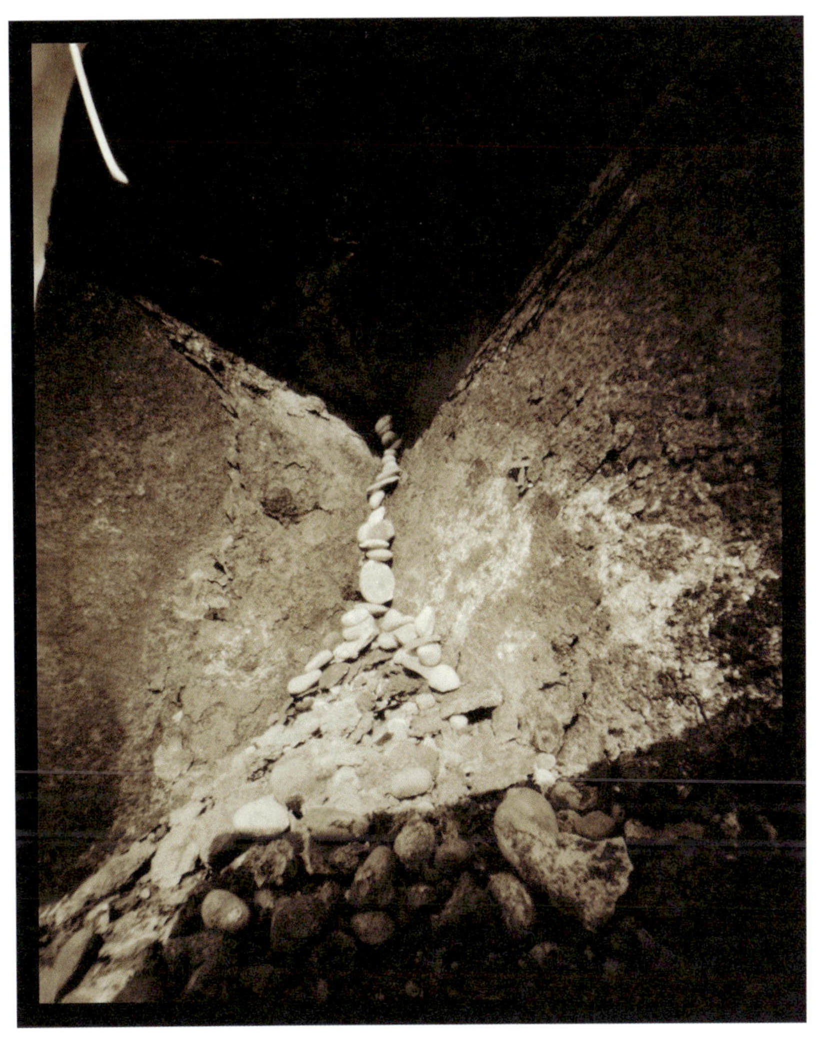

Construction XXXVII, 2003. 5 x 4 inches

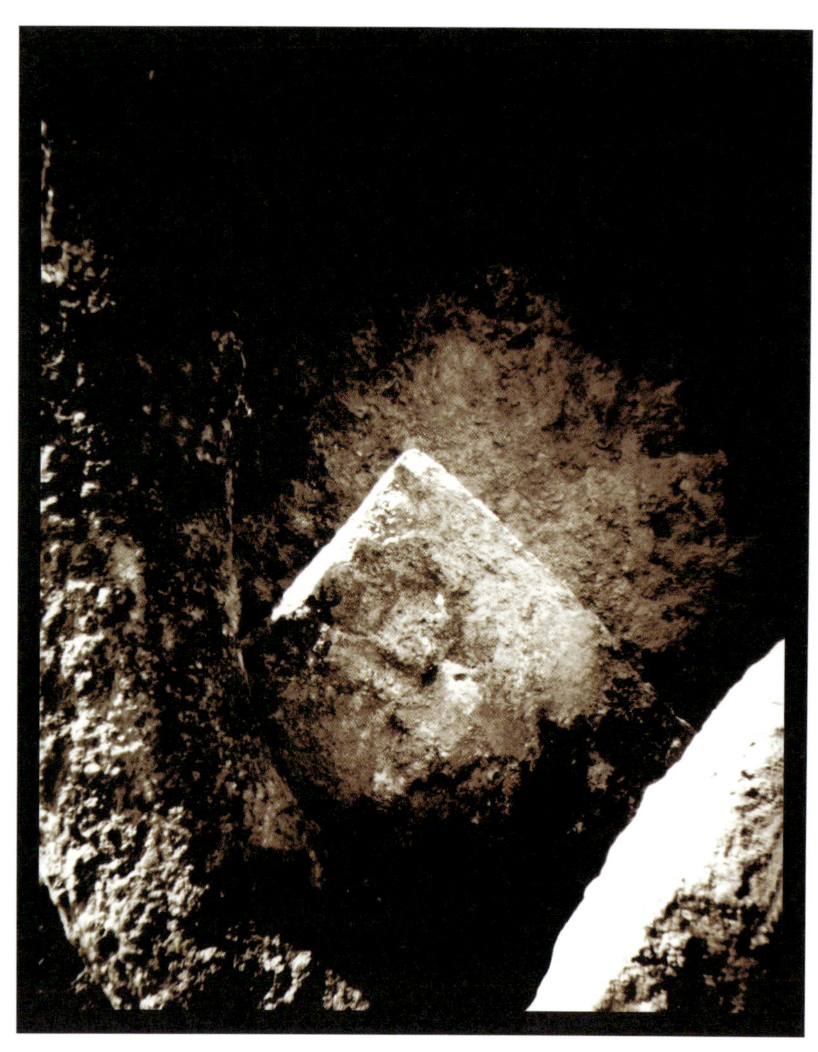

Construction XLIX, 2003. 5 x 4 inches

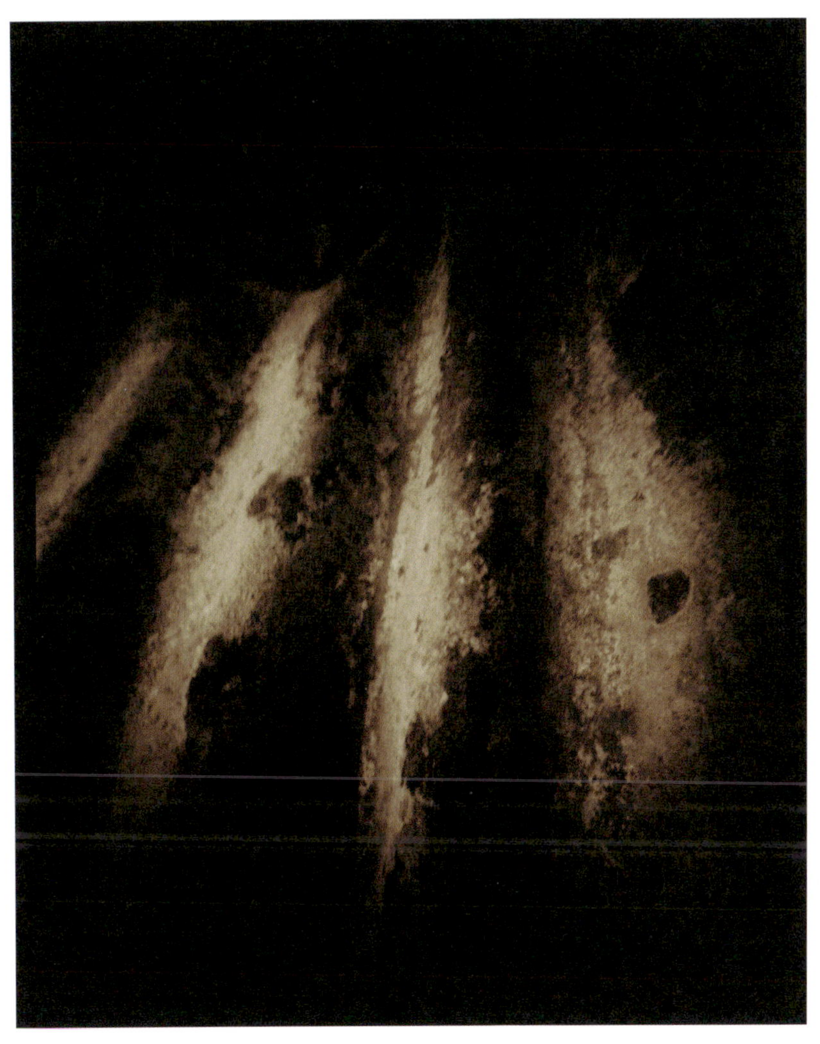

Construction XXXVI, 2003. 5 x 4 inches

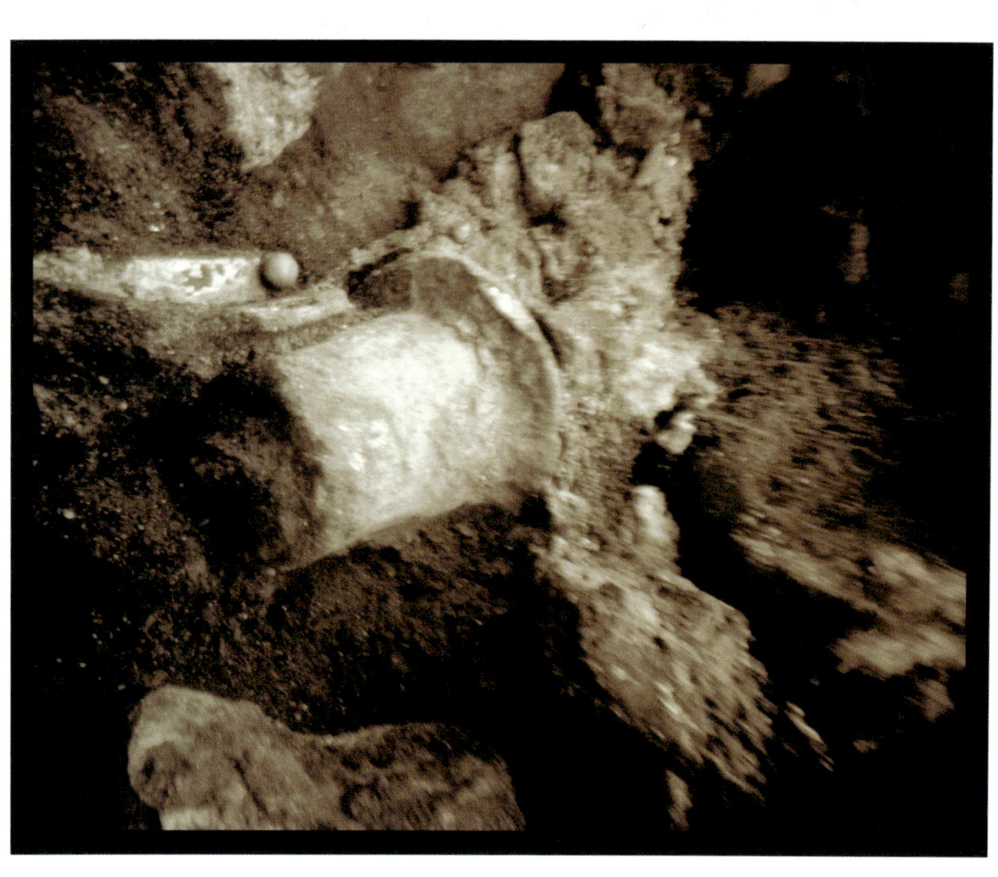

Construction LII, 2003. 4 x 5 inches

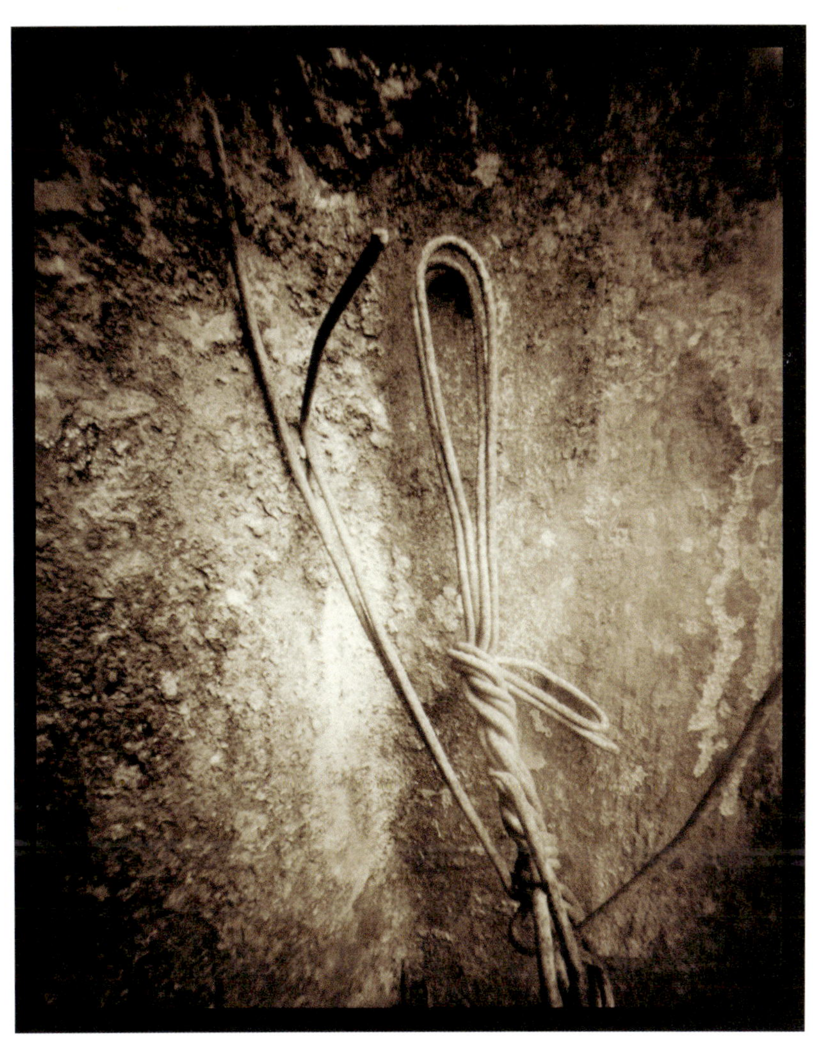

Construction XLIV, 2003. 5 x 4 inches

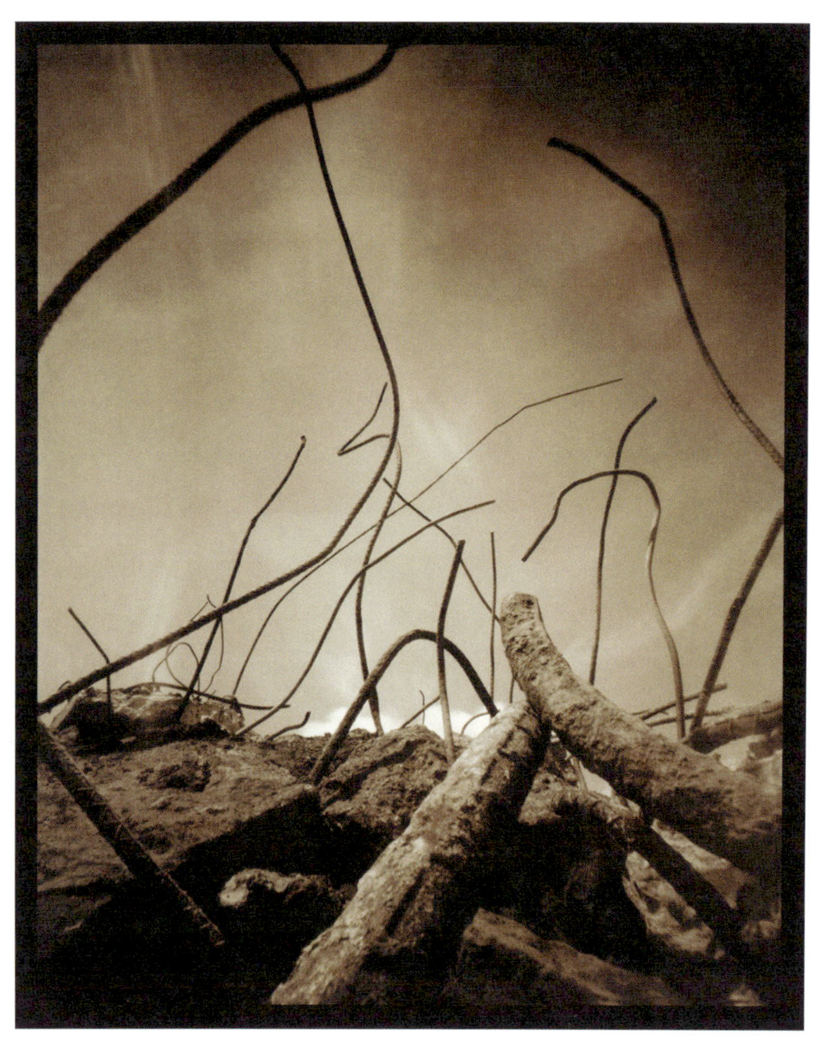

Construction V, 2003. 5 x 4 inches

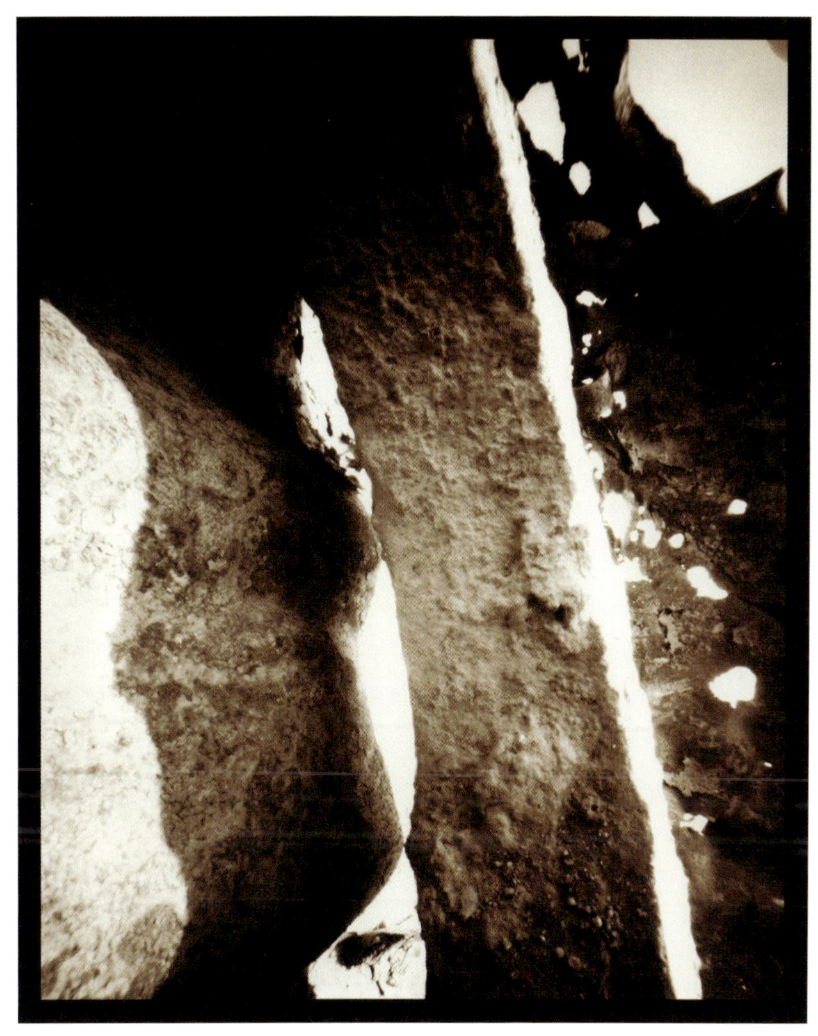

Construction XLIII, 2003. 5 x 4 inches

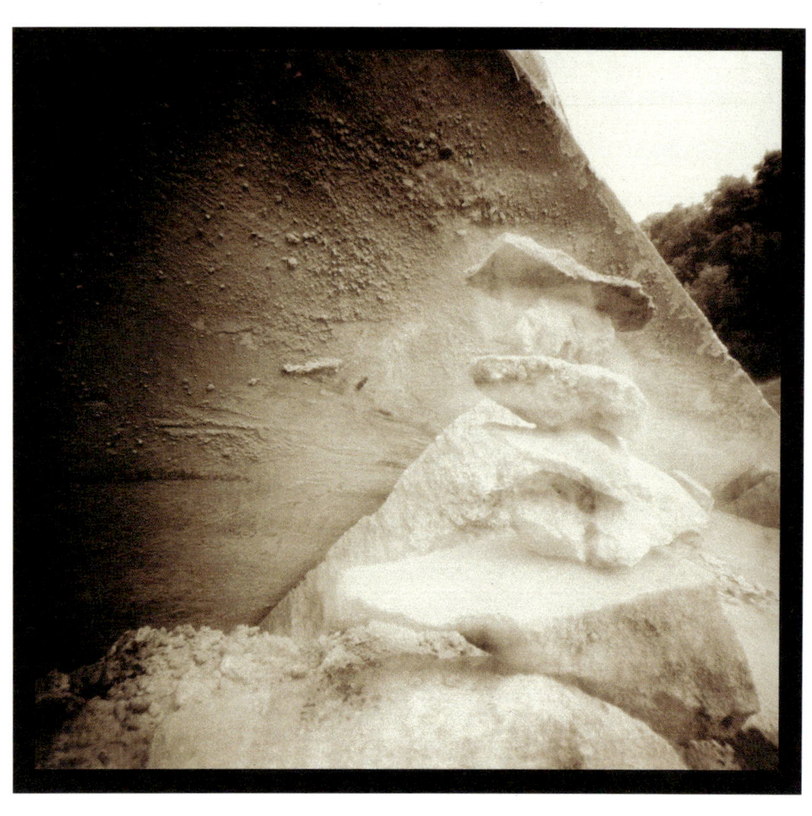

Construction XXIII, 2003. 3.75 x 4 inches

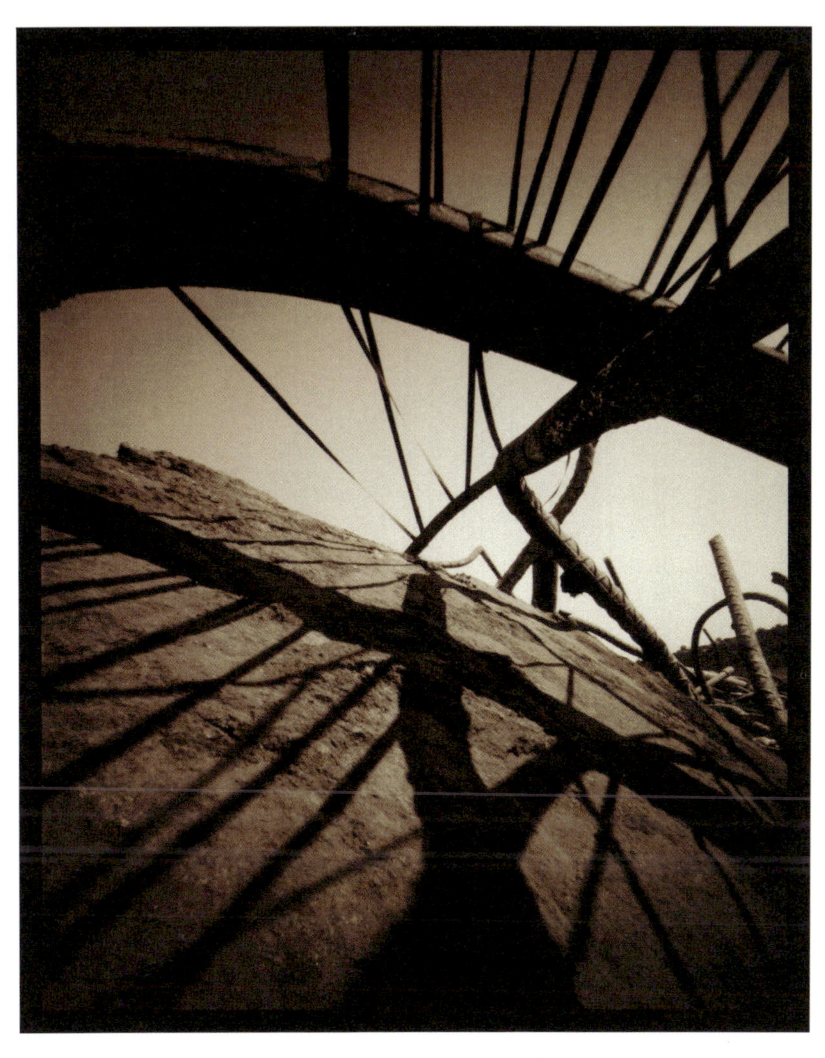

Construction XXXIX, 2003. 5 x 4 inches

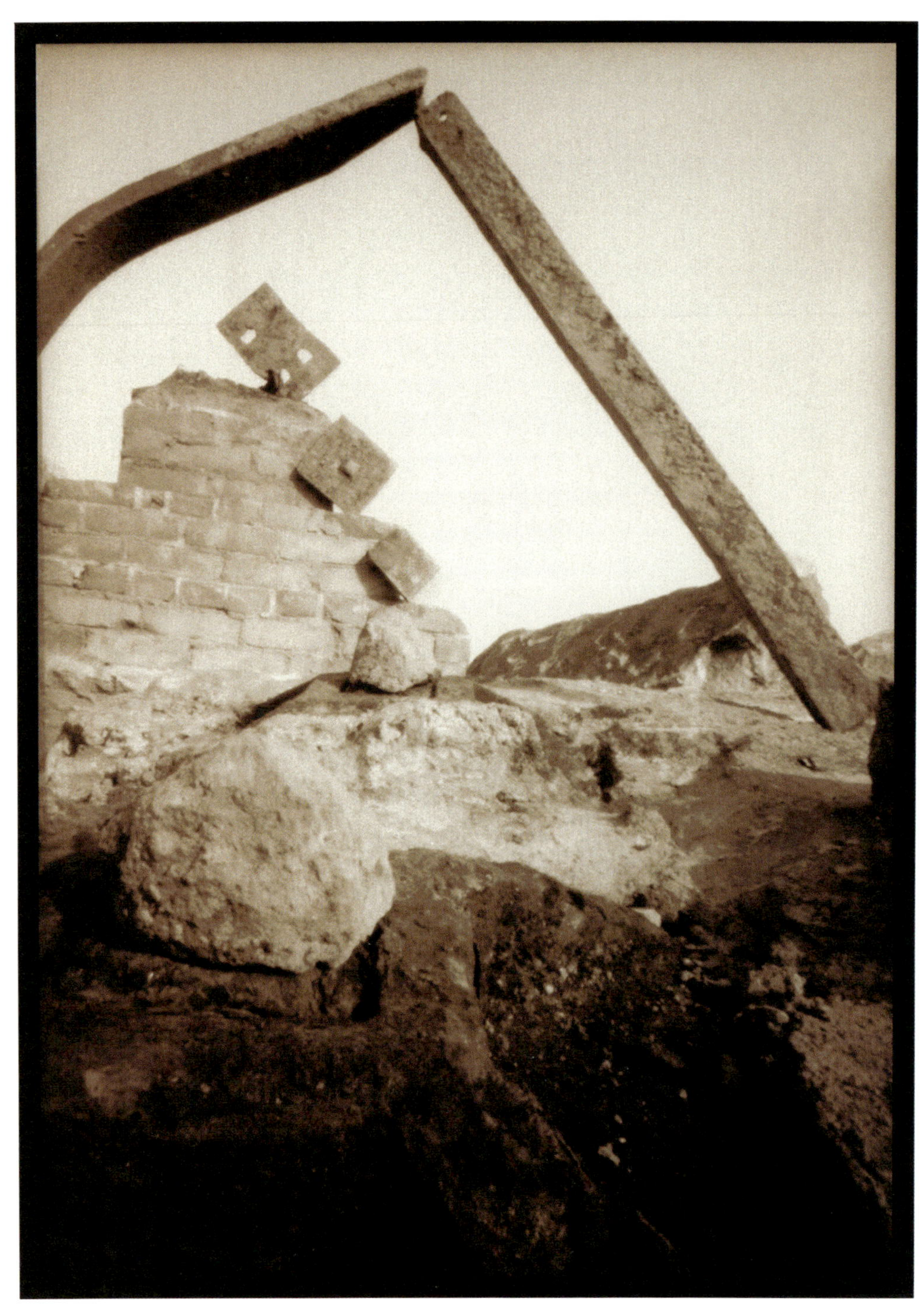

Construction XLII, 2003. 7 x 5 inches

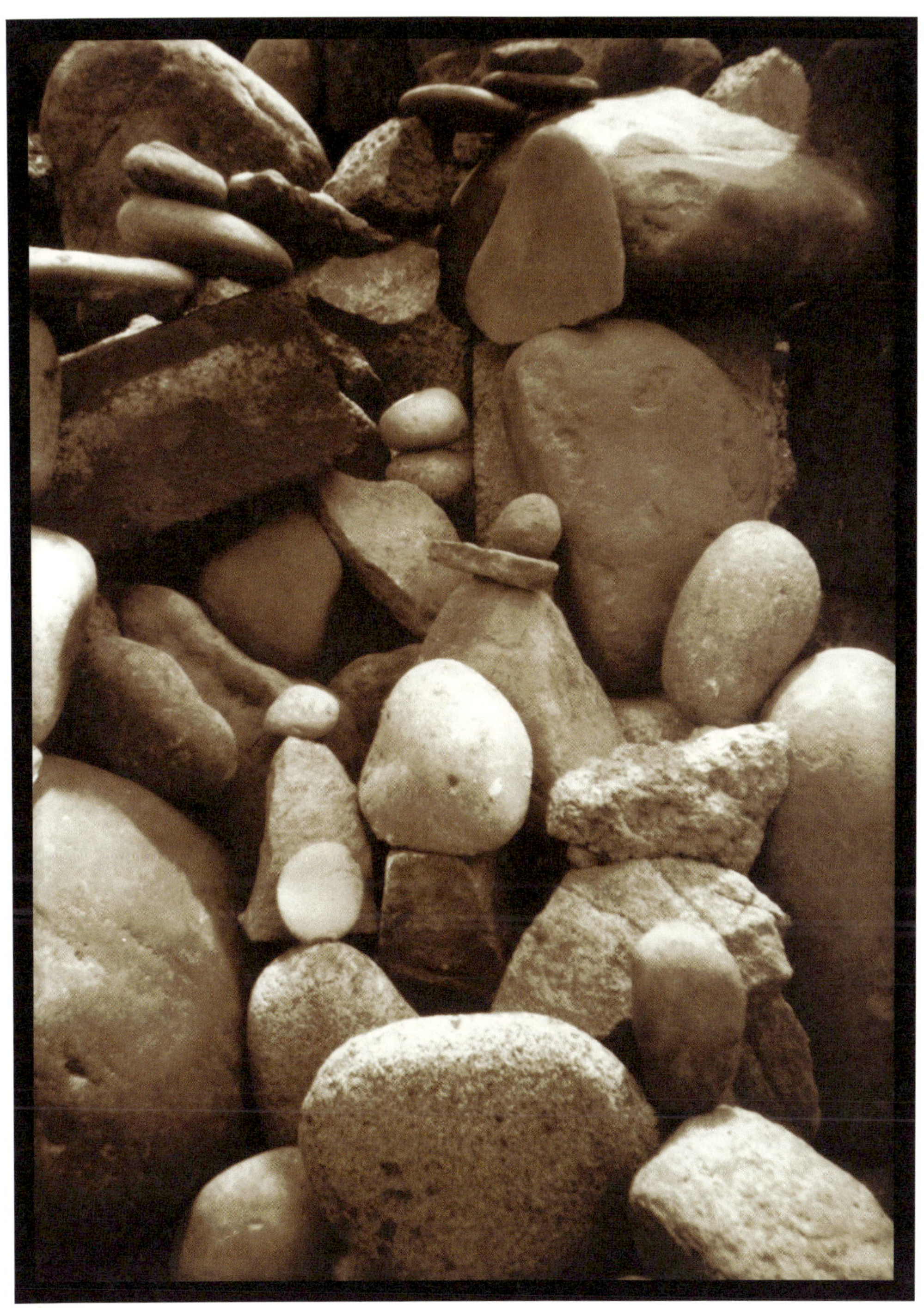

Construction XXXV, 2003. 7 x 5 inches

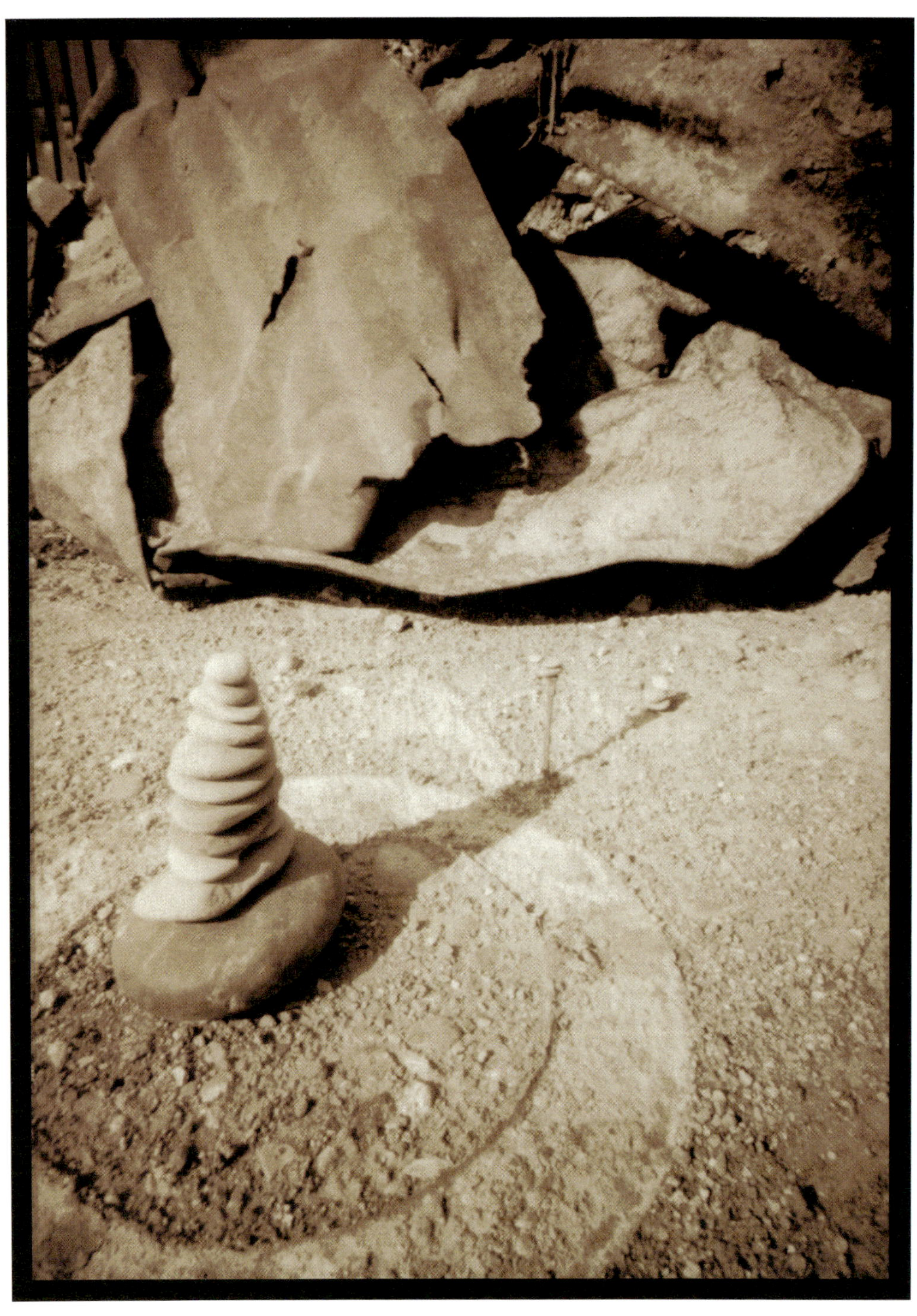

Construction XLI, 2003. 7 x 5 inches

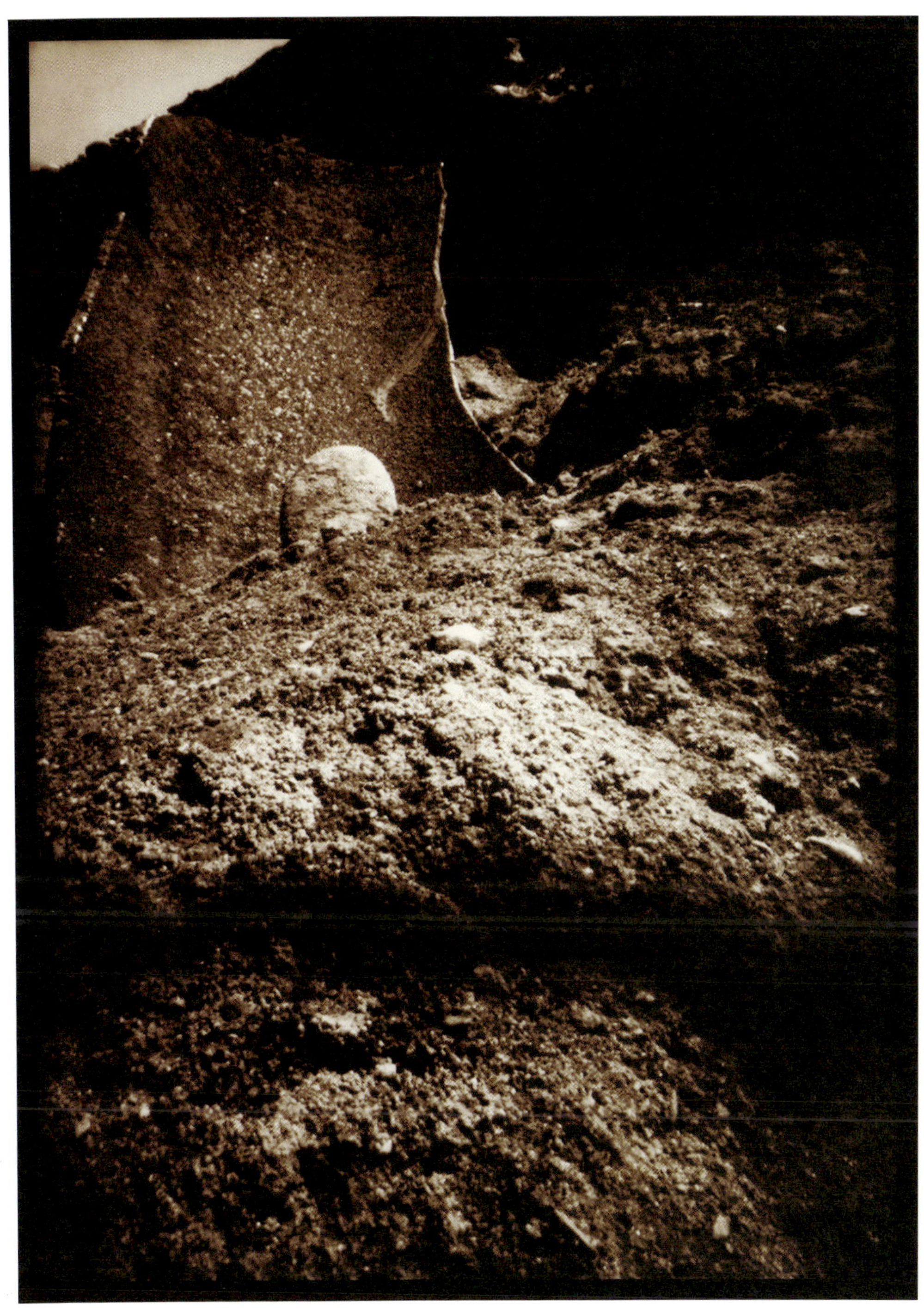

Construction XL, 2003. 7 x 5 inches

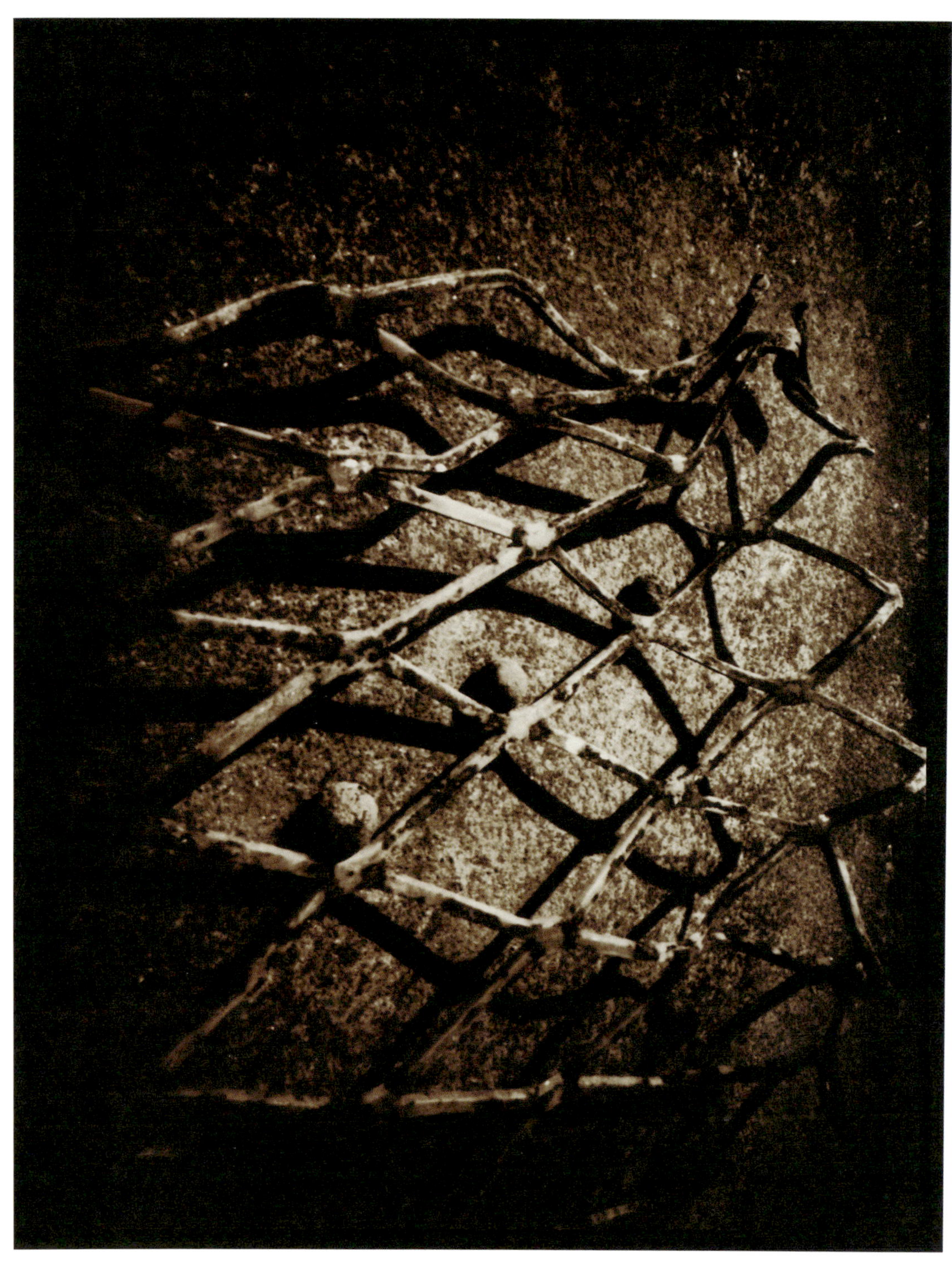

Construction LXVII, 2003. 14 x 11 inches

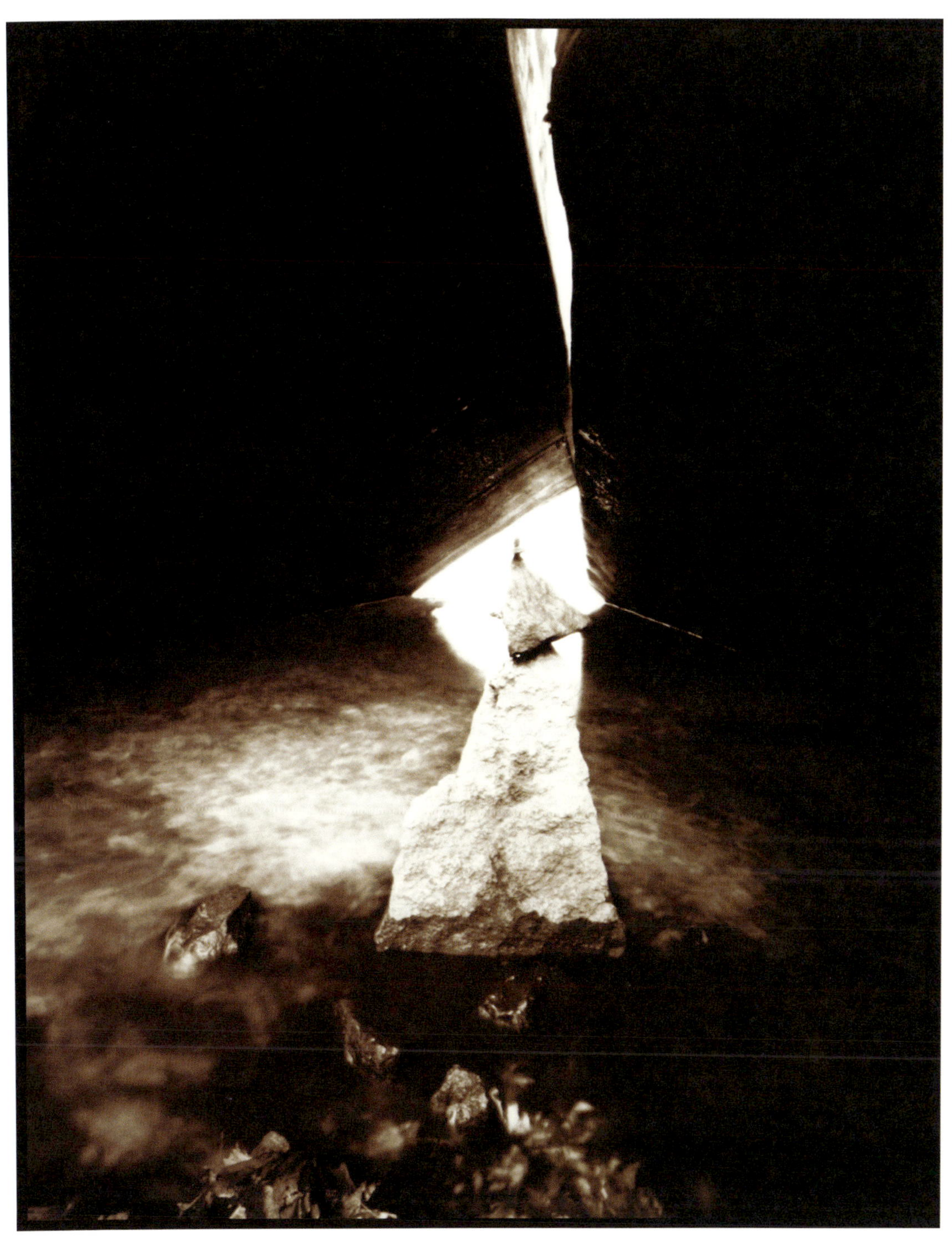

Construction LXXV, 2003. 14 x 11 inches

Structures

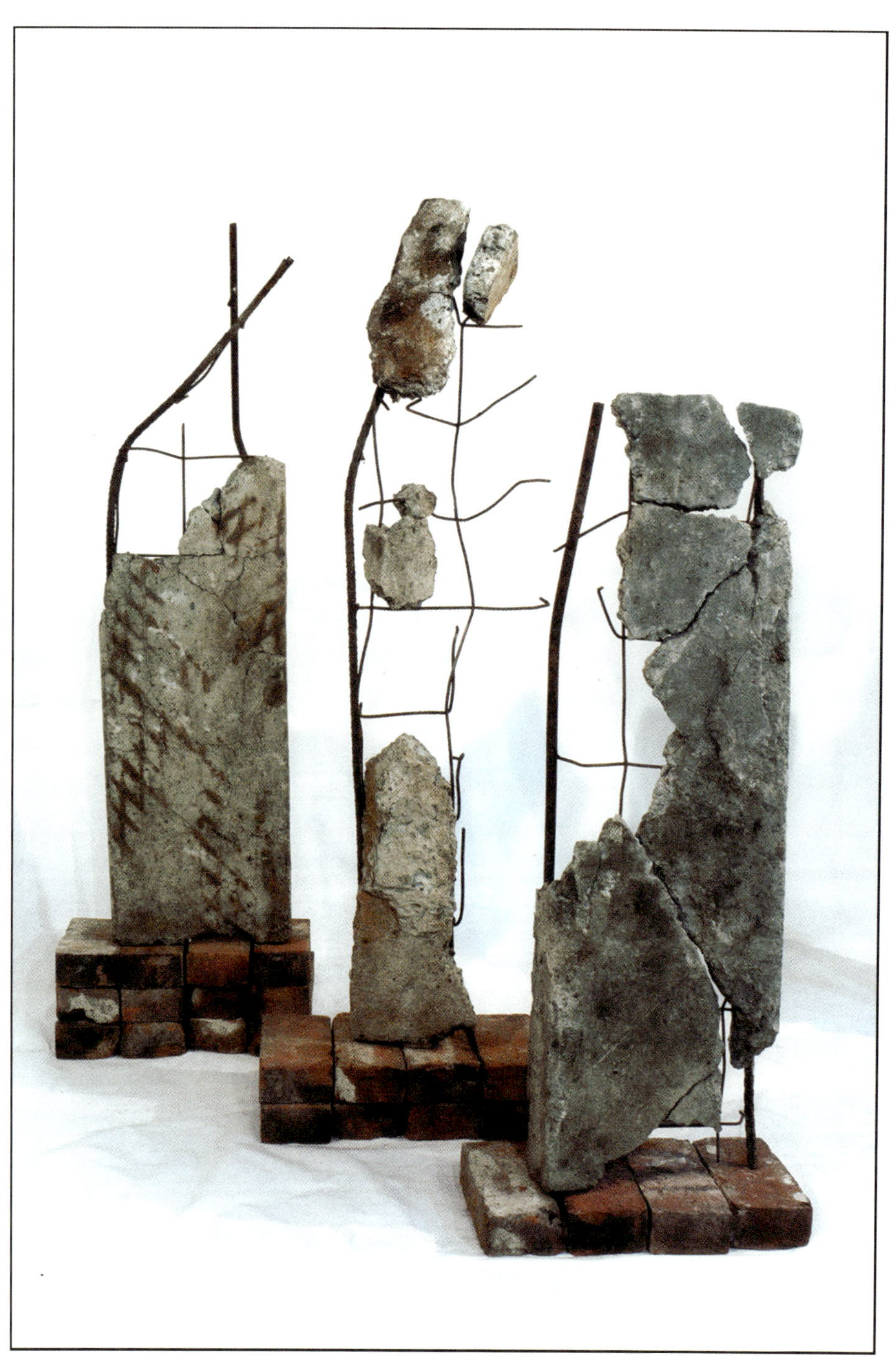

Charites, 2005
Rusting steel and cement, 54 x 40 x 34 inches

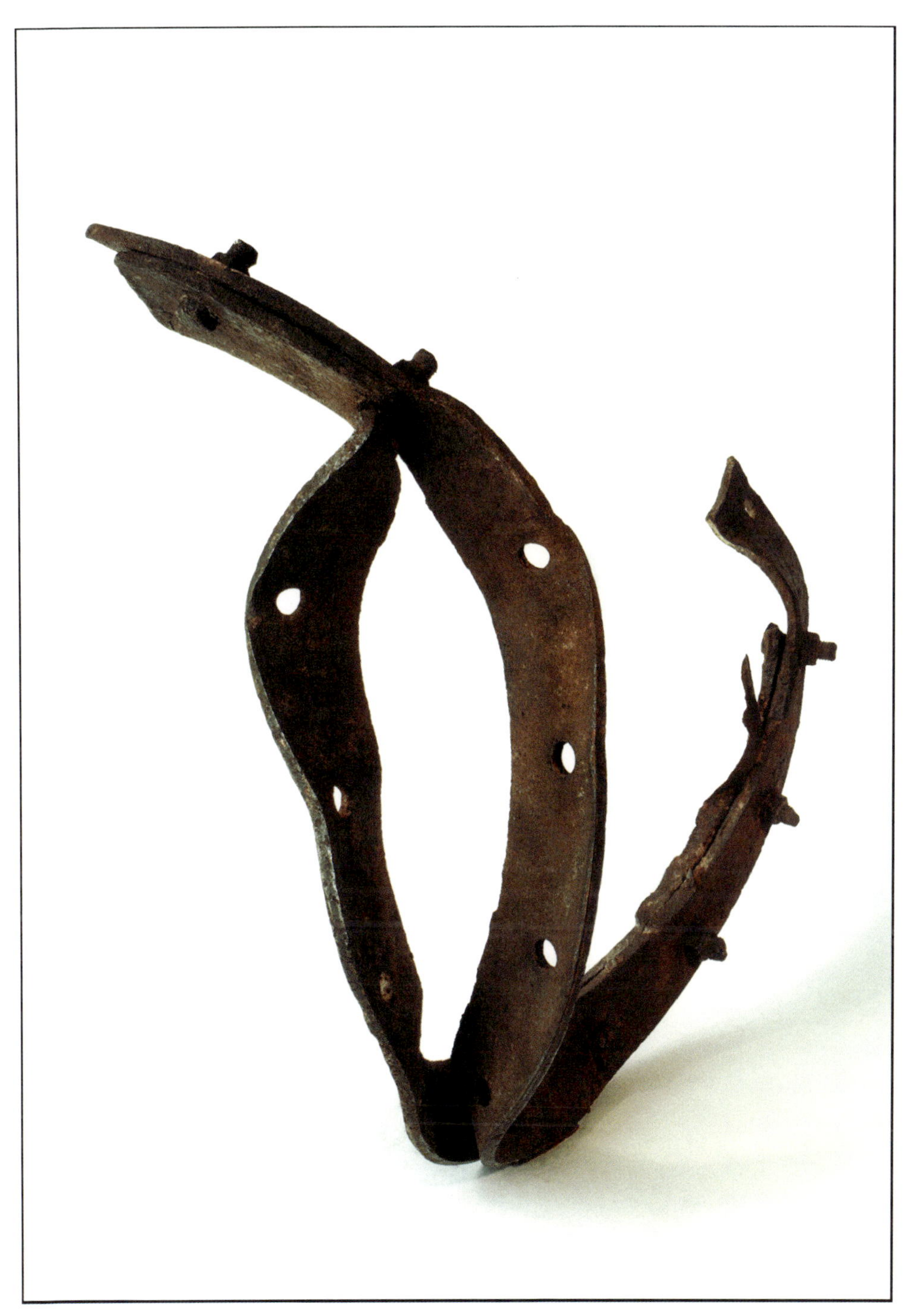

Aphrodite, 2005
Rusting steel, 25 x 14 x 24 inches

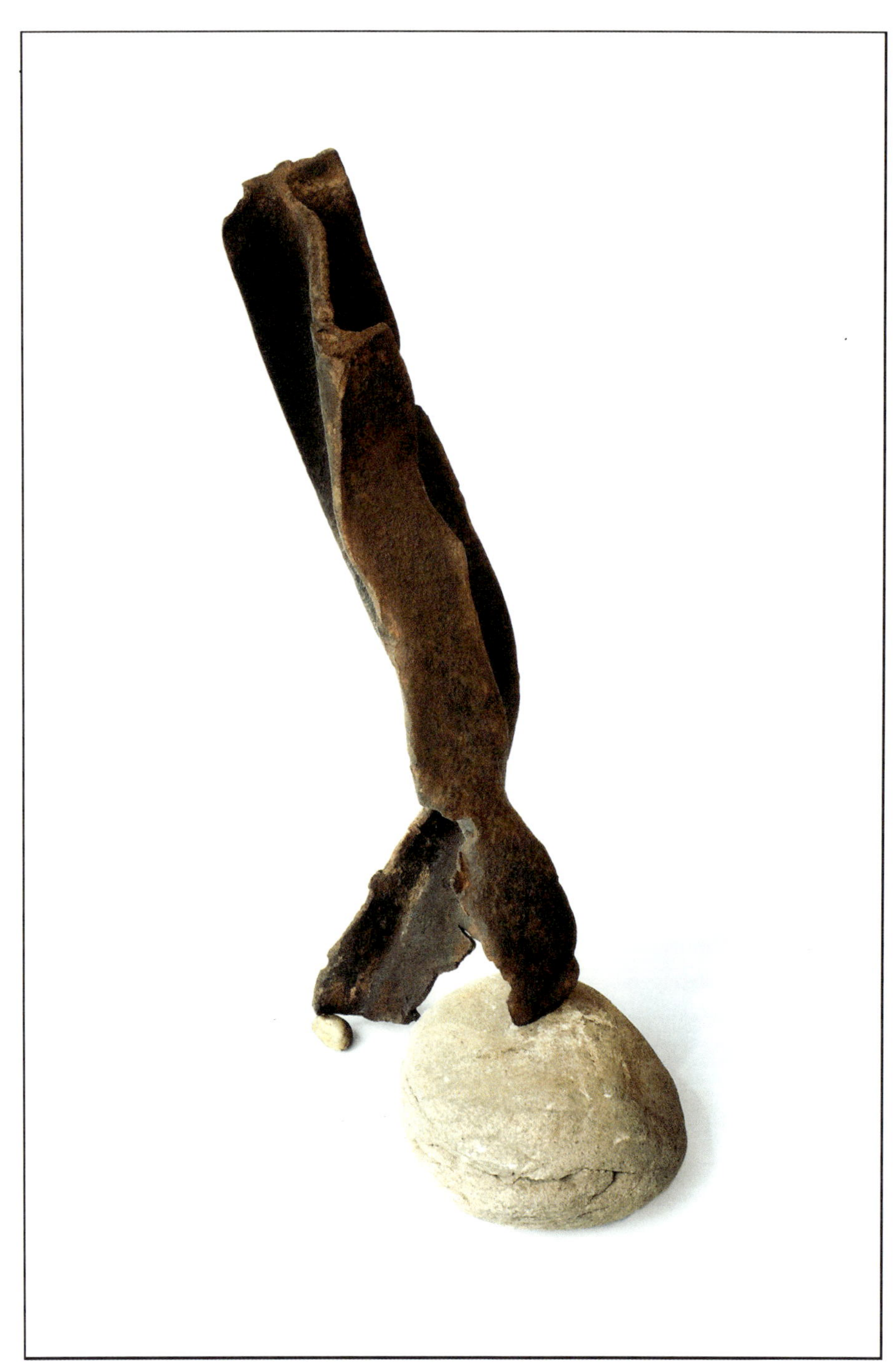

Ate, 2005
Rusting steel and stone, 27.50 x 12 x 15.50 inches

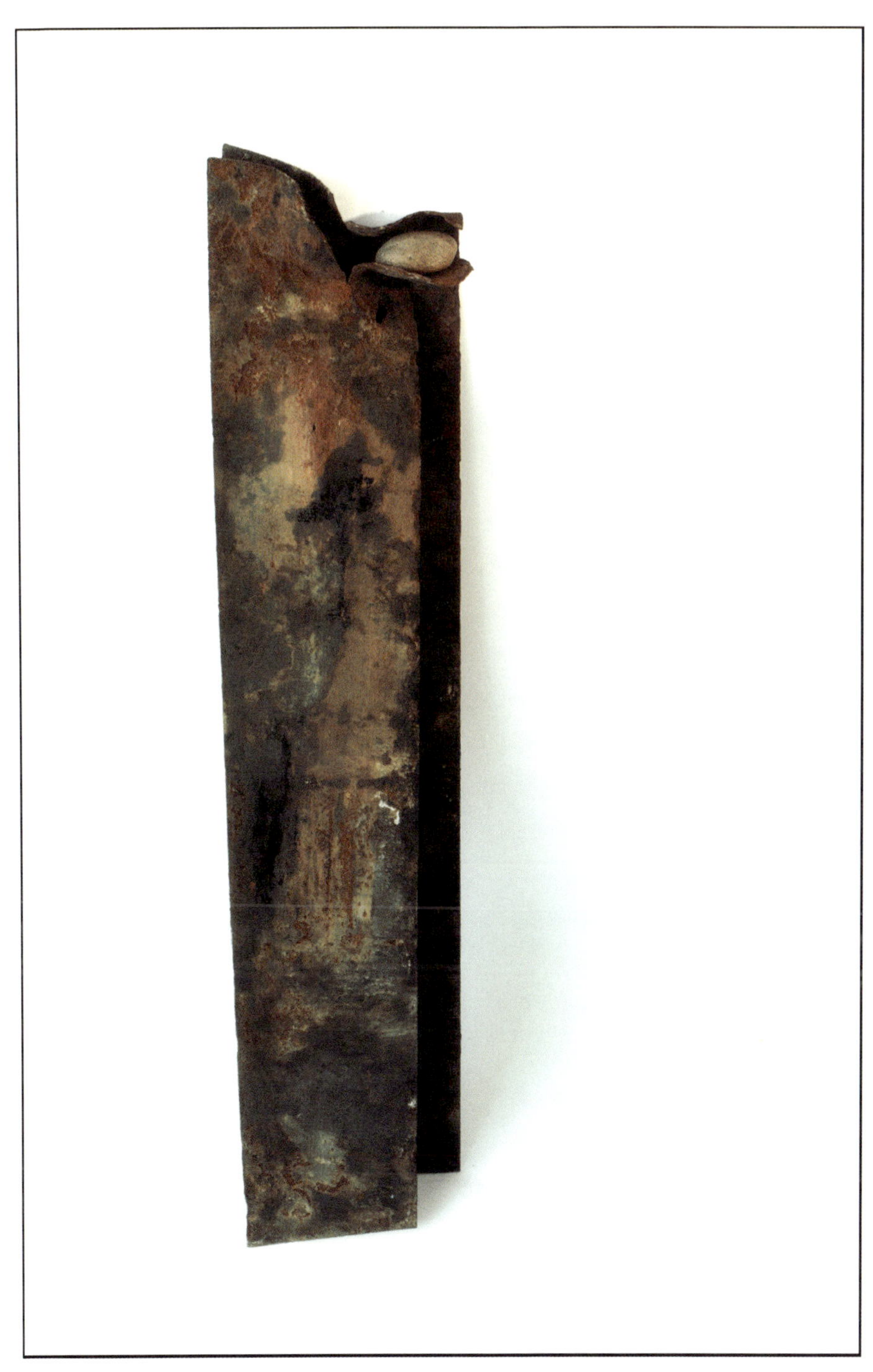

Dioscuri, 2004
Rusting steel and stone, 45.50 x 10 x 14 inches

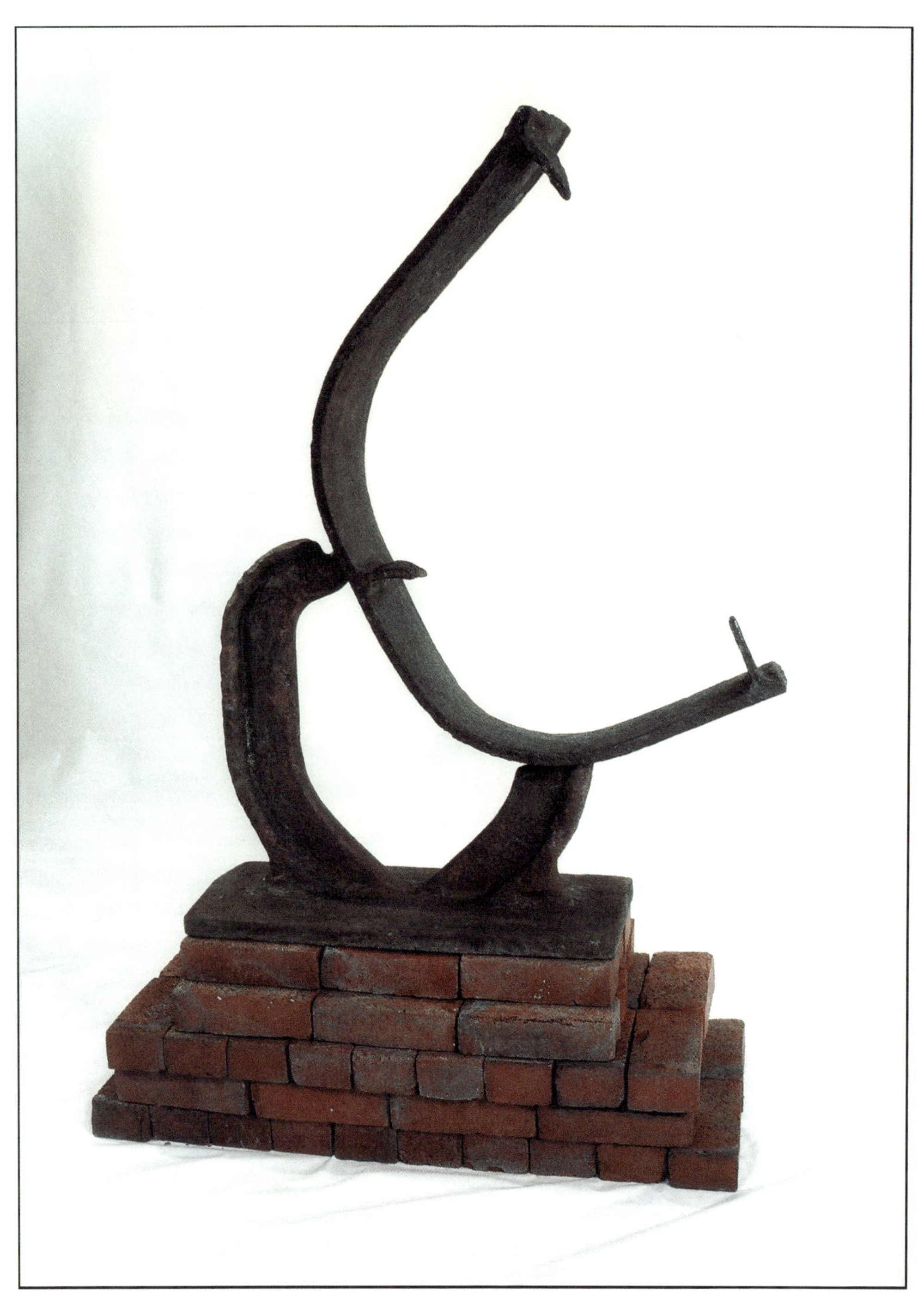

Poseidon, 2005
Rusting steel, 53 x 36 x 16.50 inches

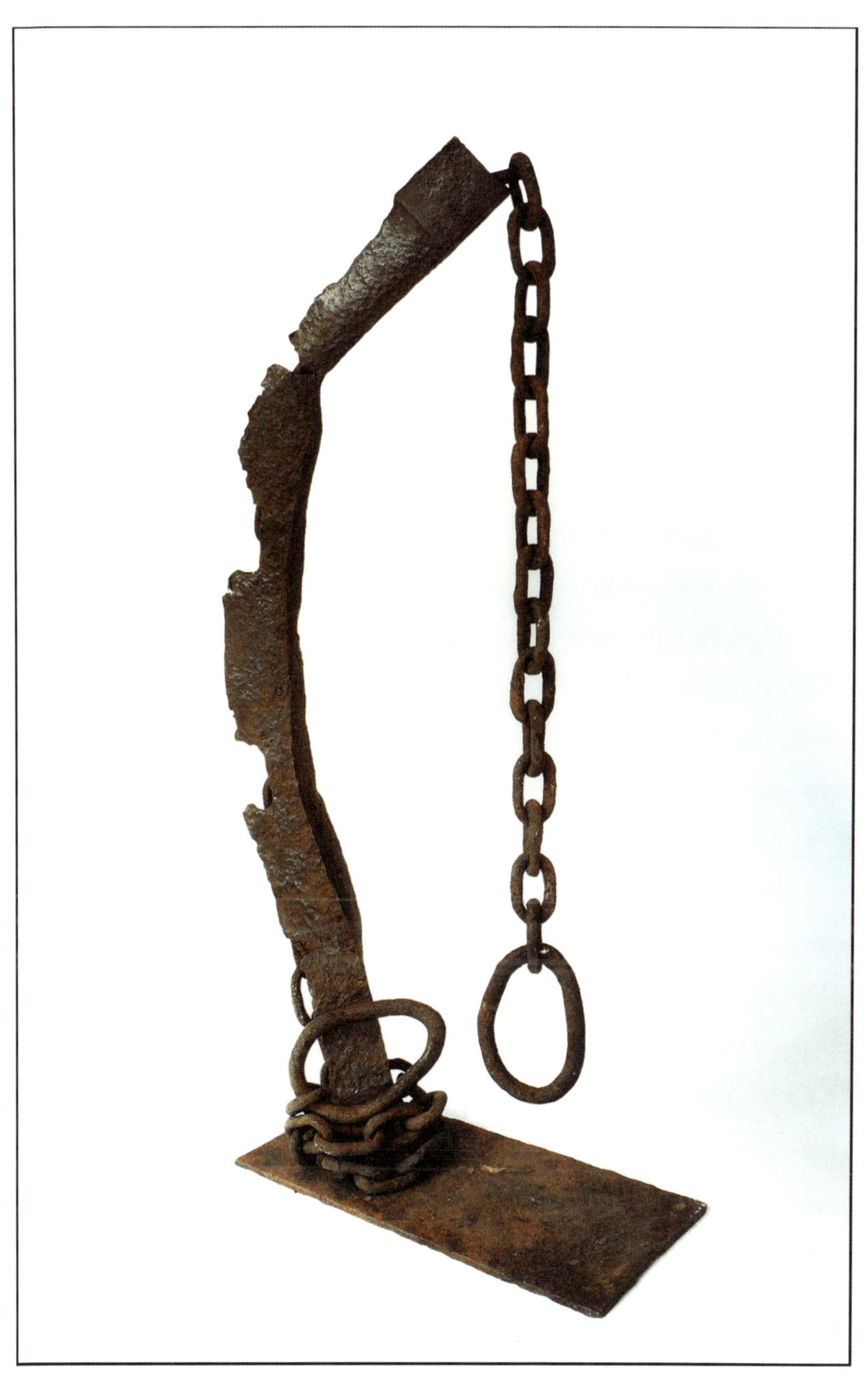

The Destiny of Queen Jocasta, 2005
Rusting steel, 39.50 x 18 x 15 inches

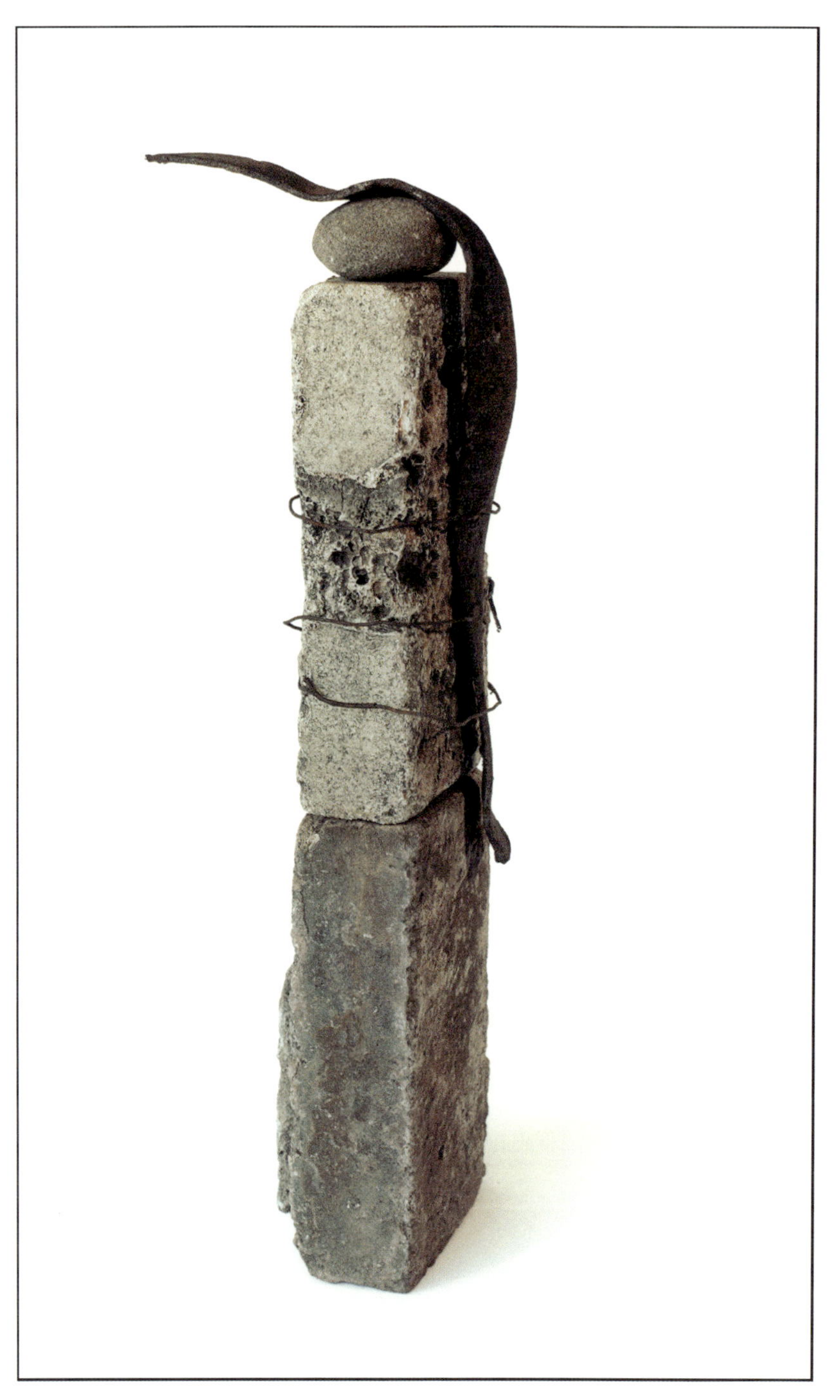

Echo, 2005
Brick, rusting steel, wire and stone, 21 x 6 x 5 inches

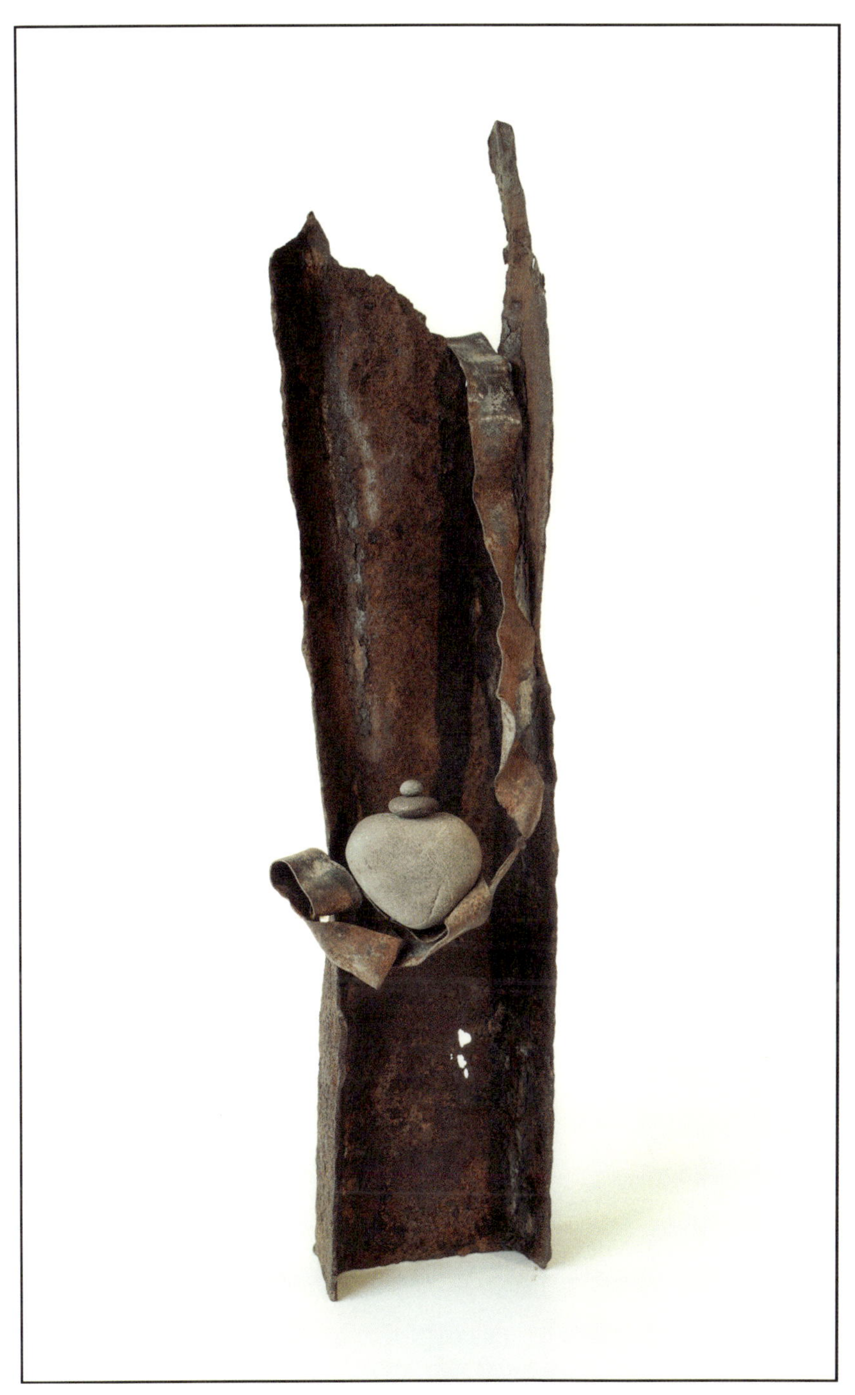

Homonoia, 2005
Rusting steel and stone, 25 x 5 x 3.50 inches

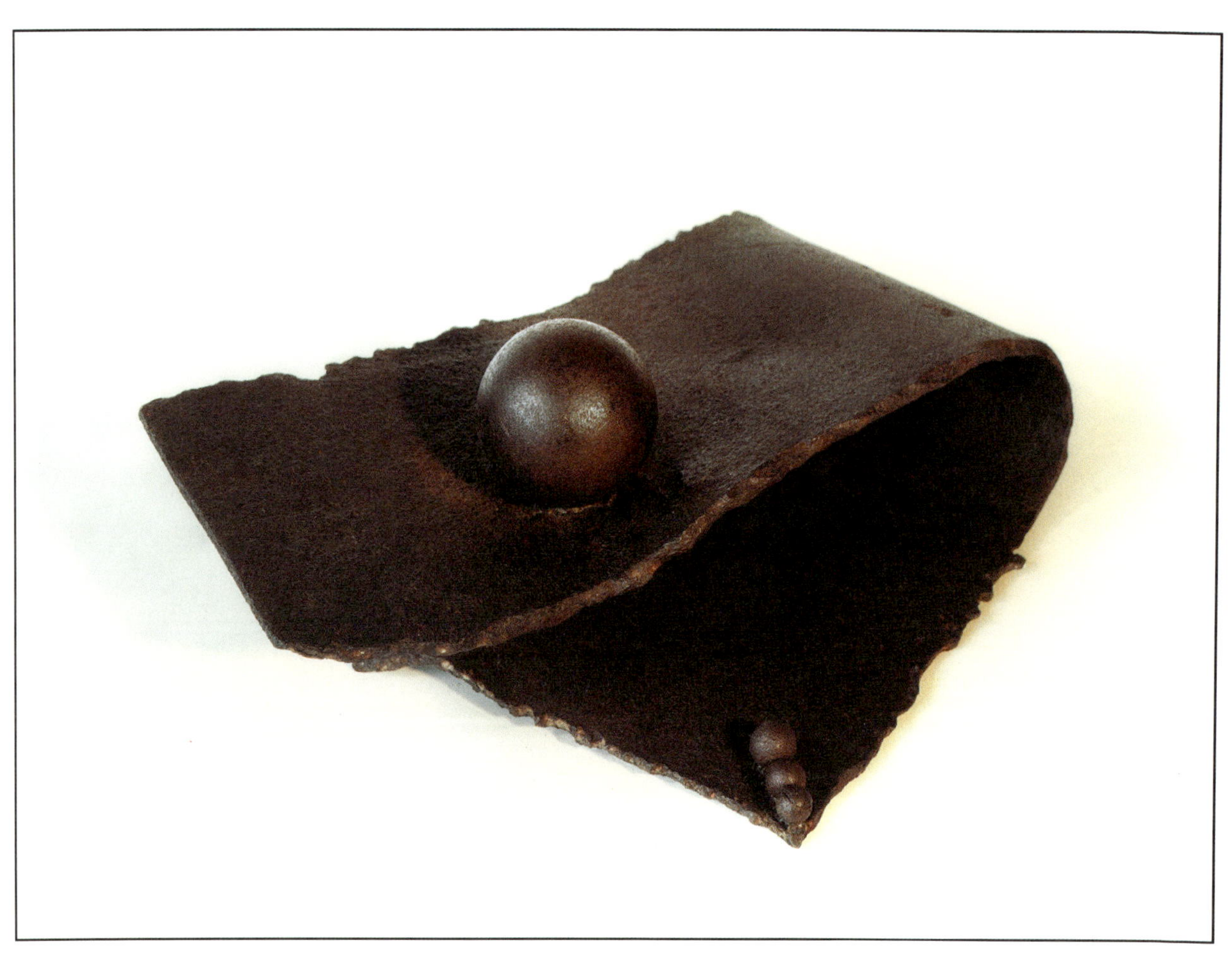

Lethe and the Three Graces, 2003
Rusting steel, 4.50 x 13 x 9.50 inches

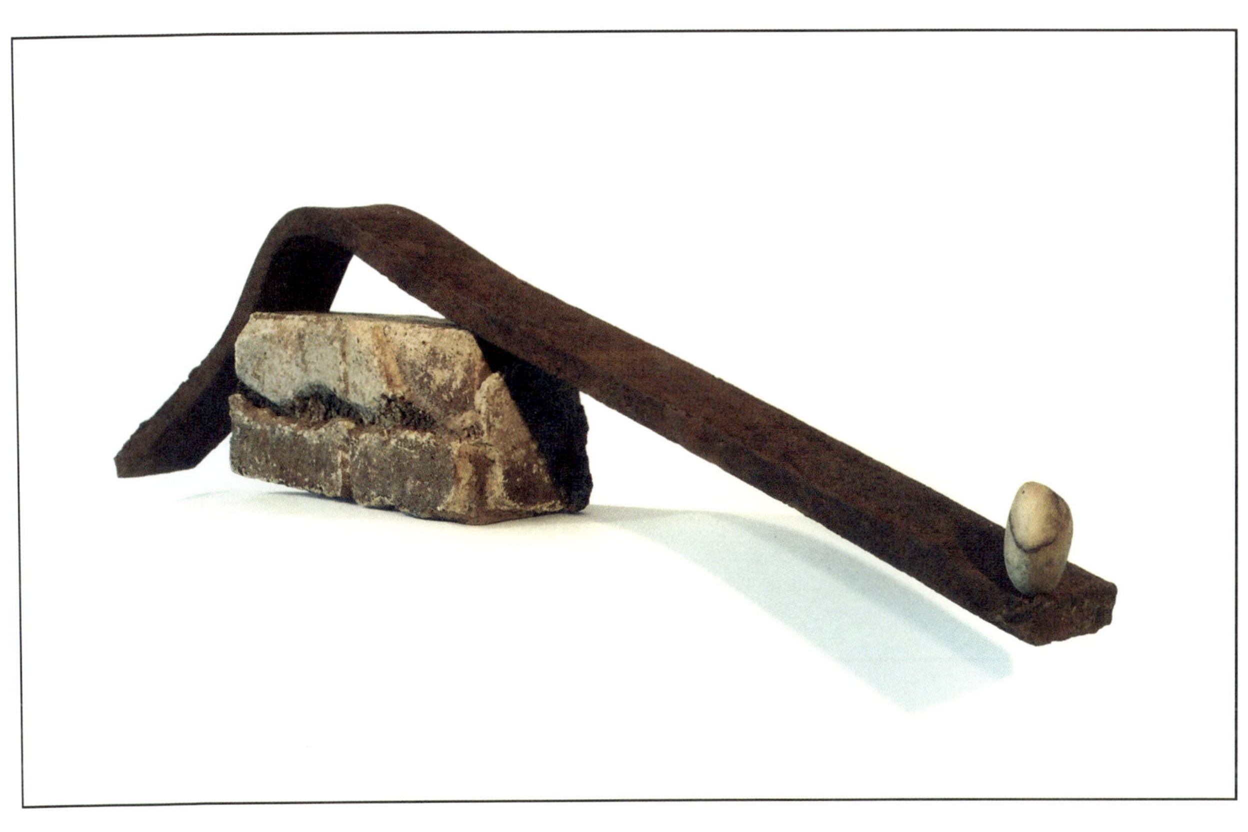

Sisyphus, 2005
Brick, rusting steel and stone, 6.50 x 31.50 x 3.50 inches

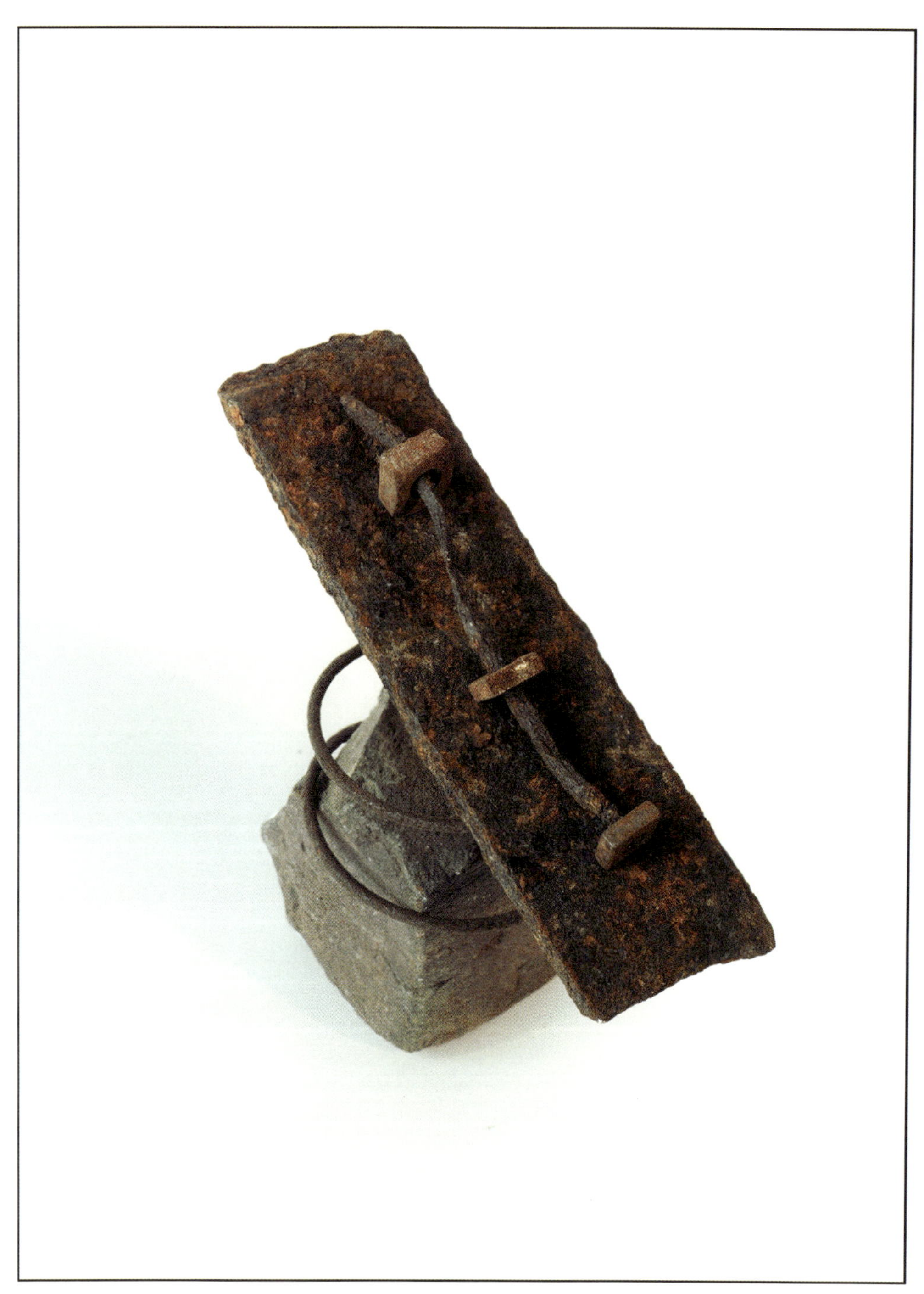

Horae, 2005
Rusting steel and stone, 4.75 x 2.25 x 5.50 inches

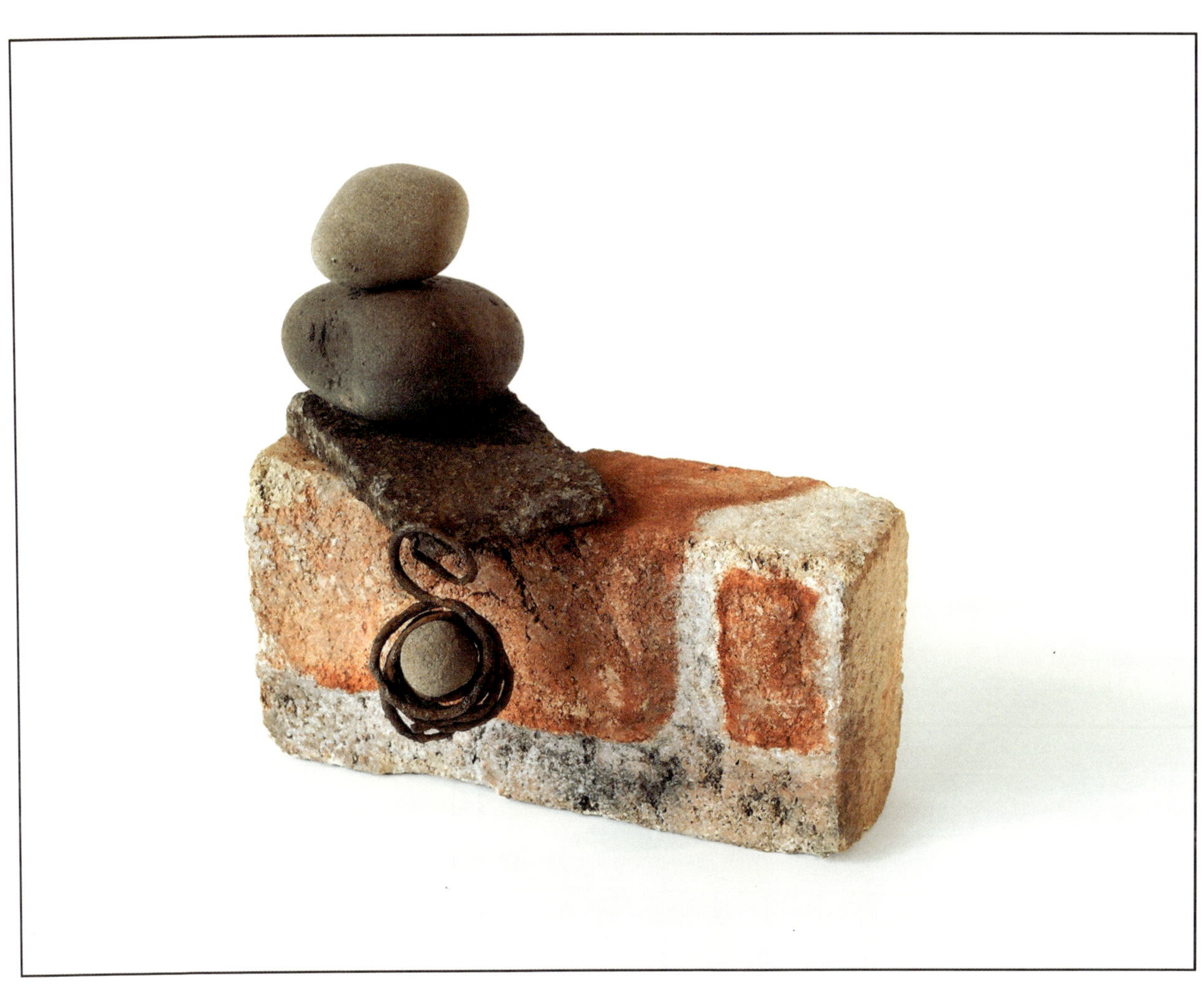

Iphis and Anaxarete, 2003
Brick, rusting steel and stone, 8.50 x 9 x 6 inches

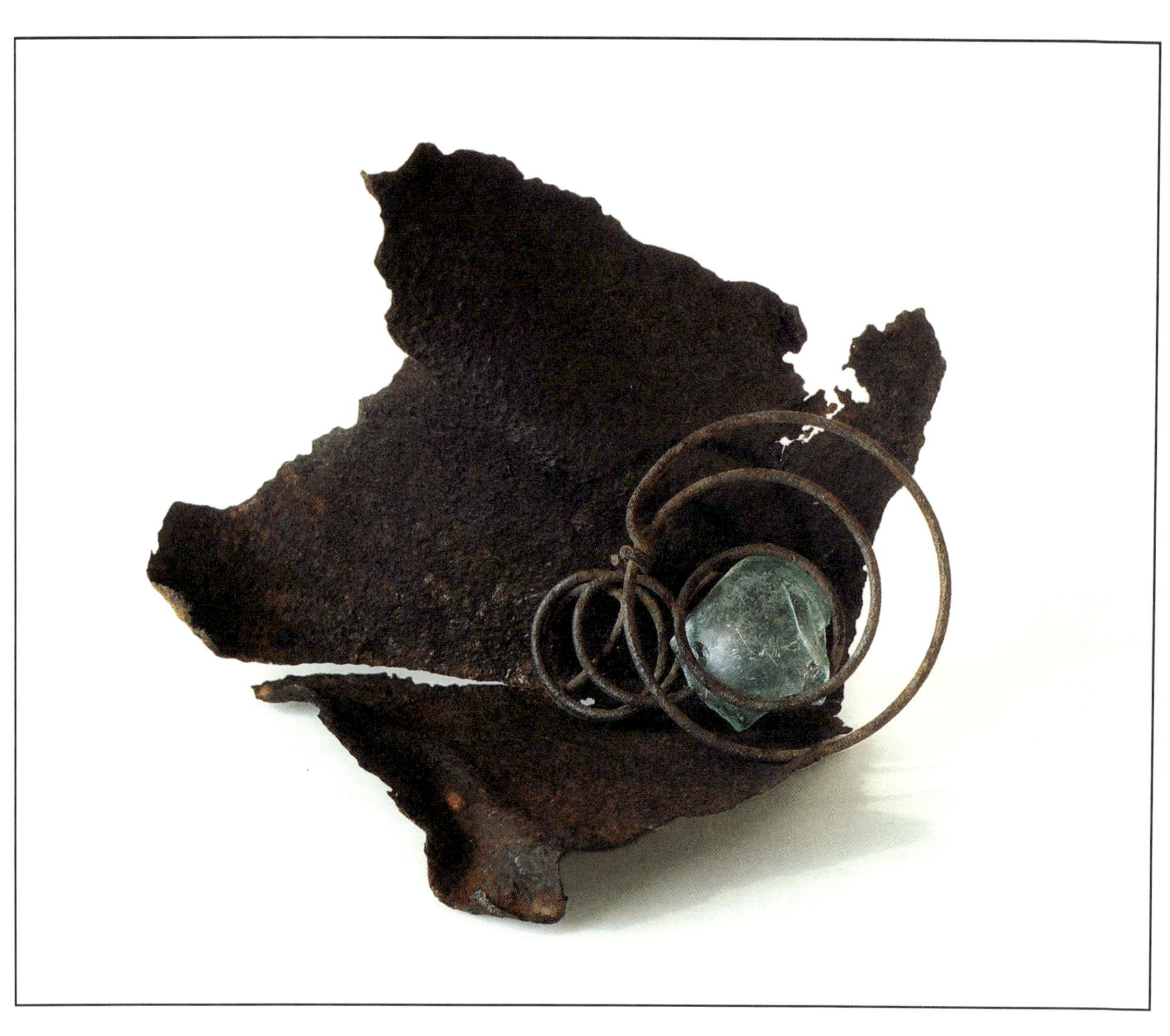

The Sirens Moan, 2005
Rusting steel and glass, 7.25 x 11 x 8 inches

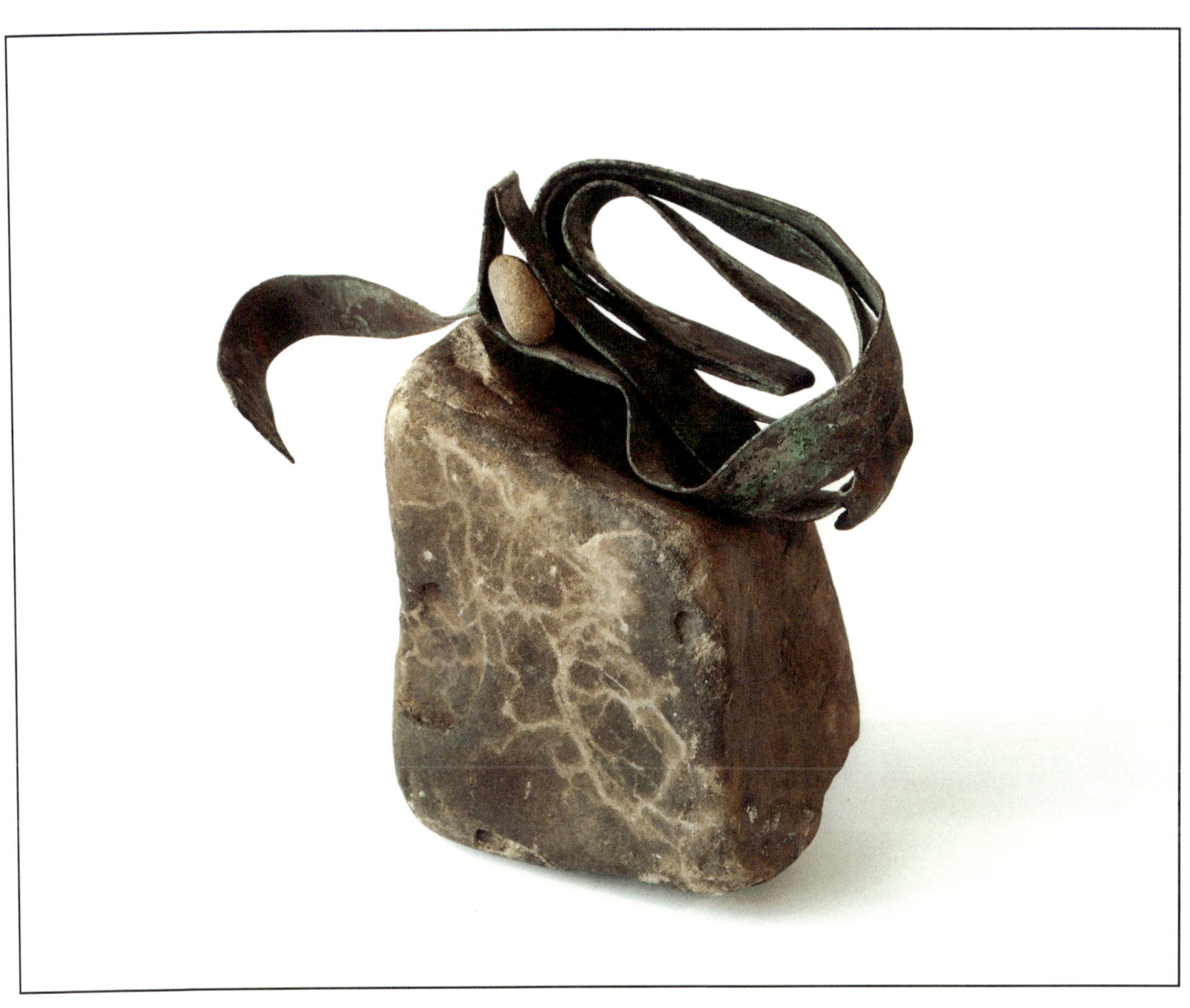

Amphitrite, 2003
Rock, copper and stone, 10.50 x 10.50 x 5.50 inches

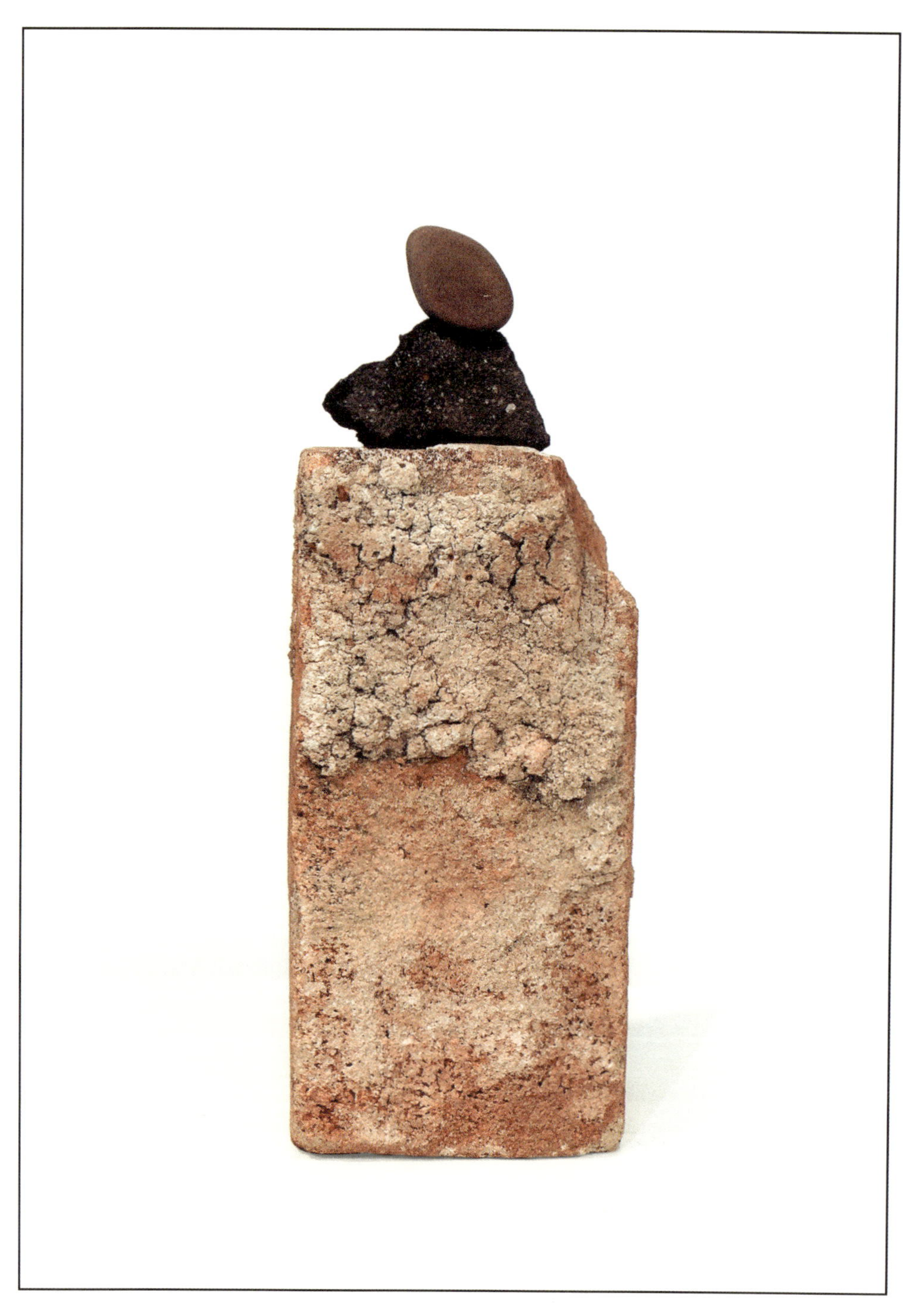

Structure for Mount Olympus, 2003
Brick, asphalt and stone, 11.50 x 4.25 x 2.75 inches

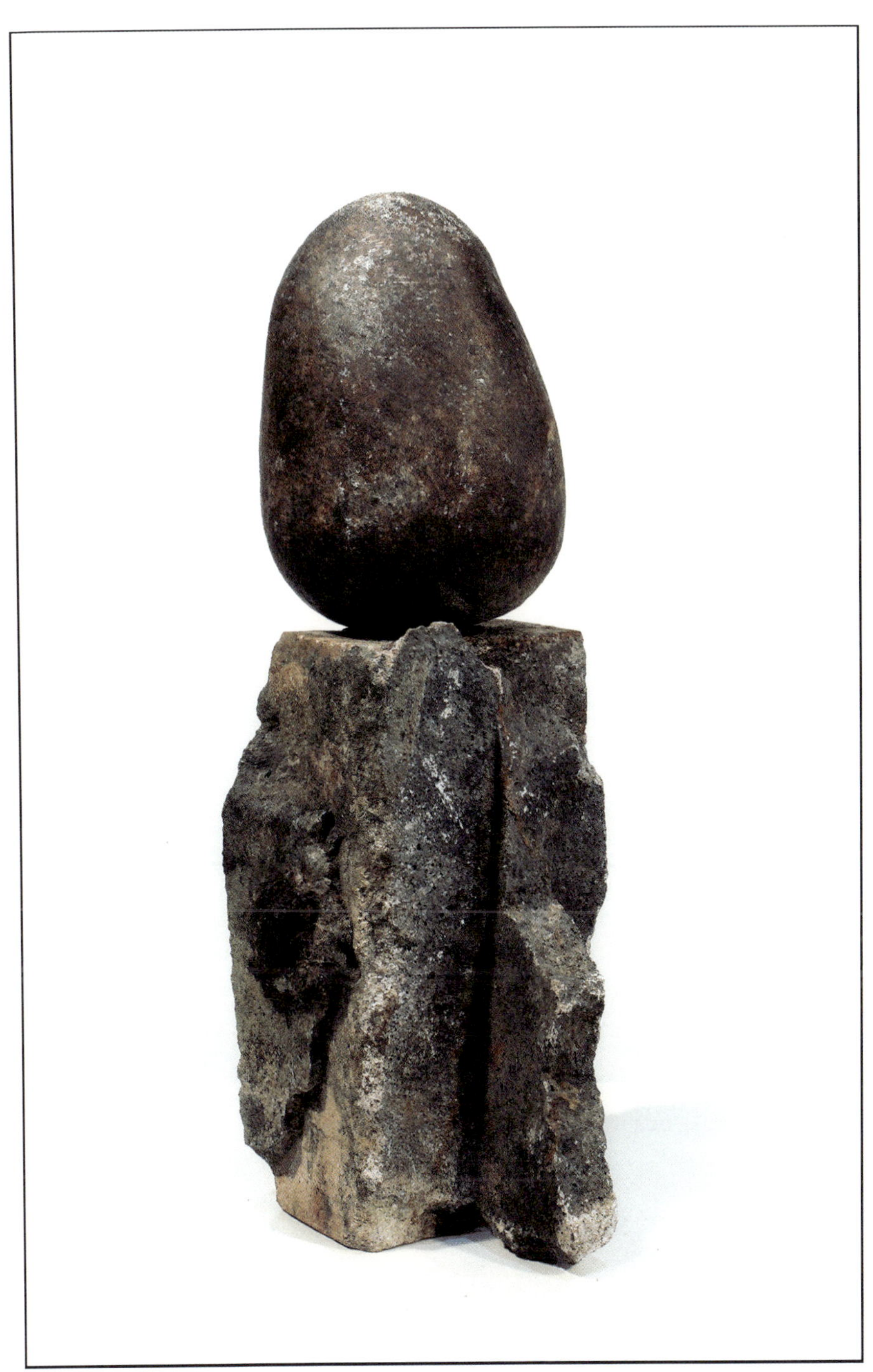

Priapus, 2003
Brick and stone, 15 x 7 x 6 inches

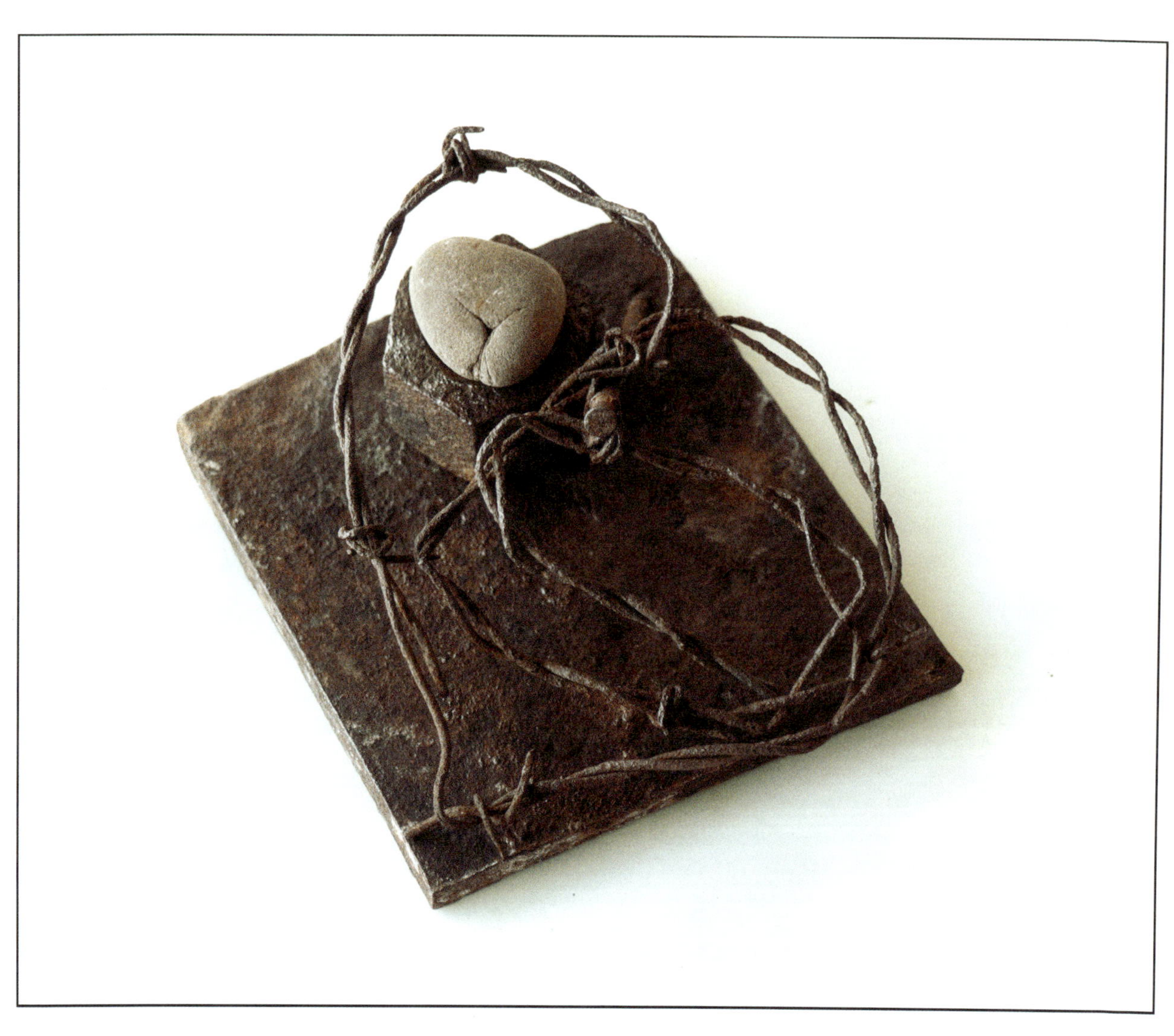

Artemis, 2005
Rusting steel and stone, 2.75 x 7.50 x 6 inches

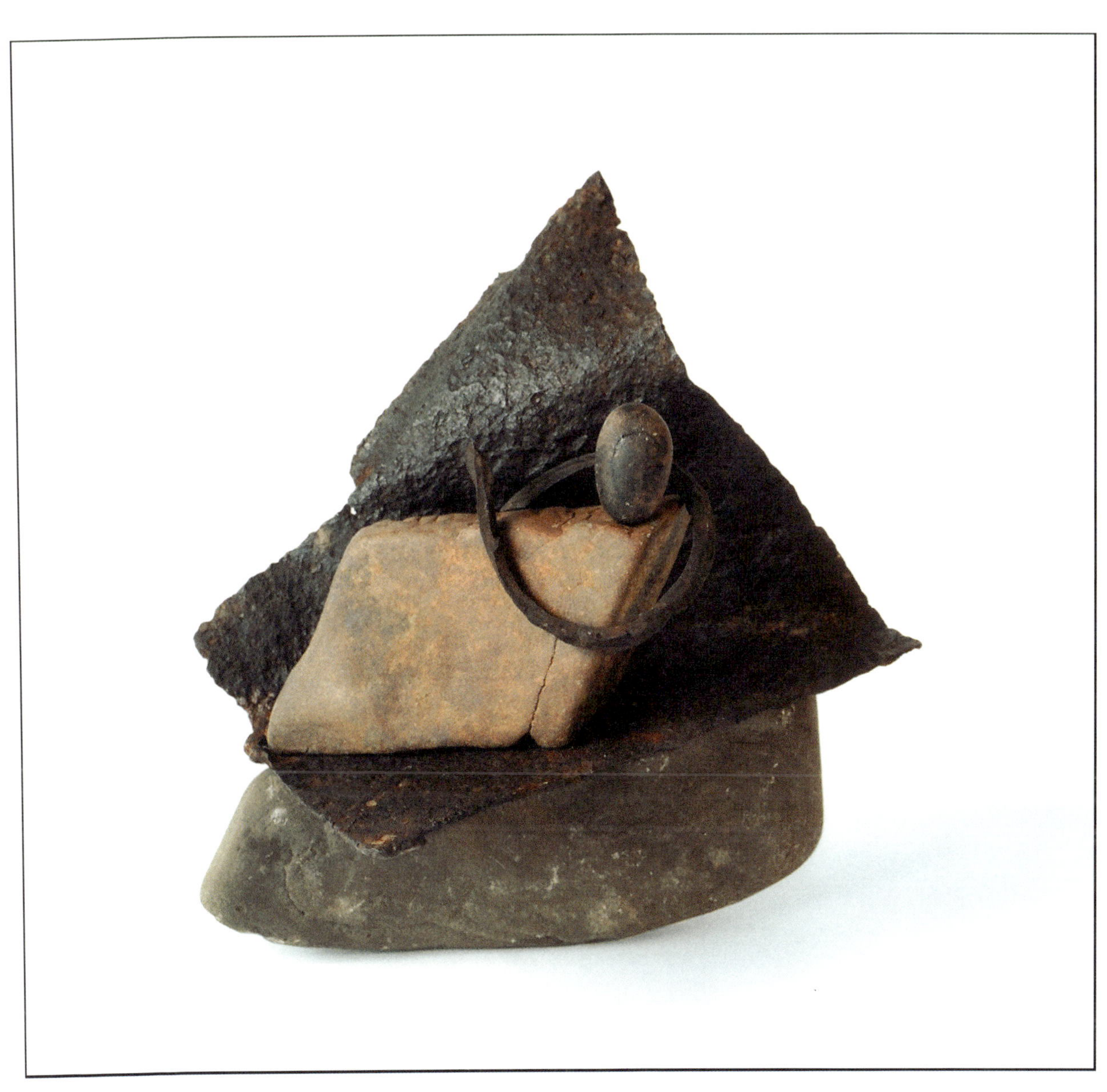

Deucalion and Pyrra, 2005
Rusting steel and stone, 9.25 x 10 x 10 inches

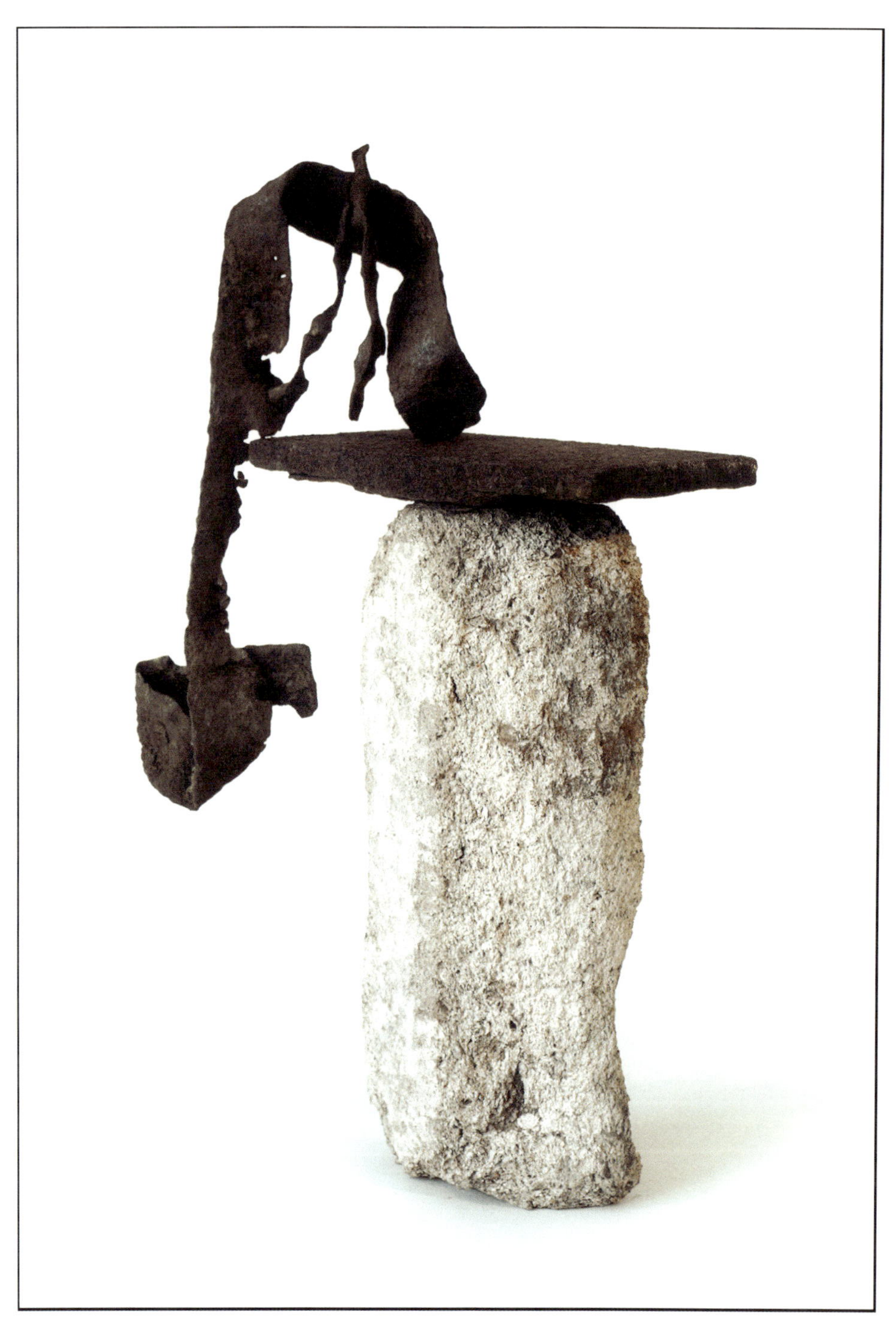

Nemesis, 2005
Brick and rusting steel, 14 x 9.75 x 5 inches

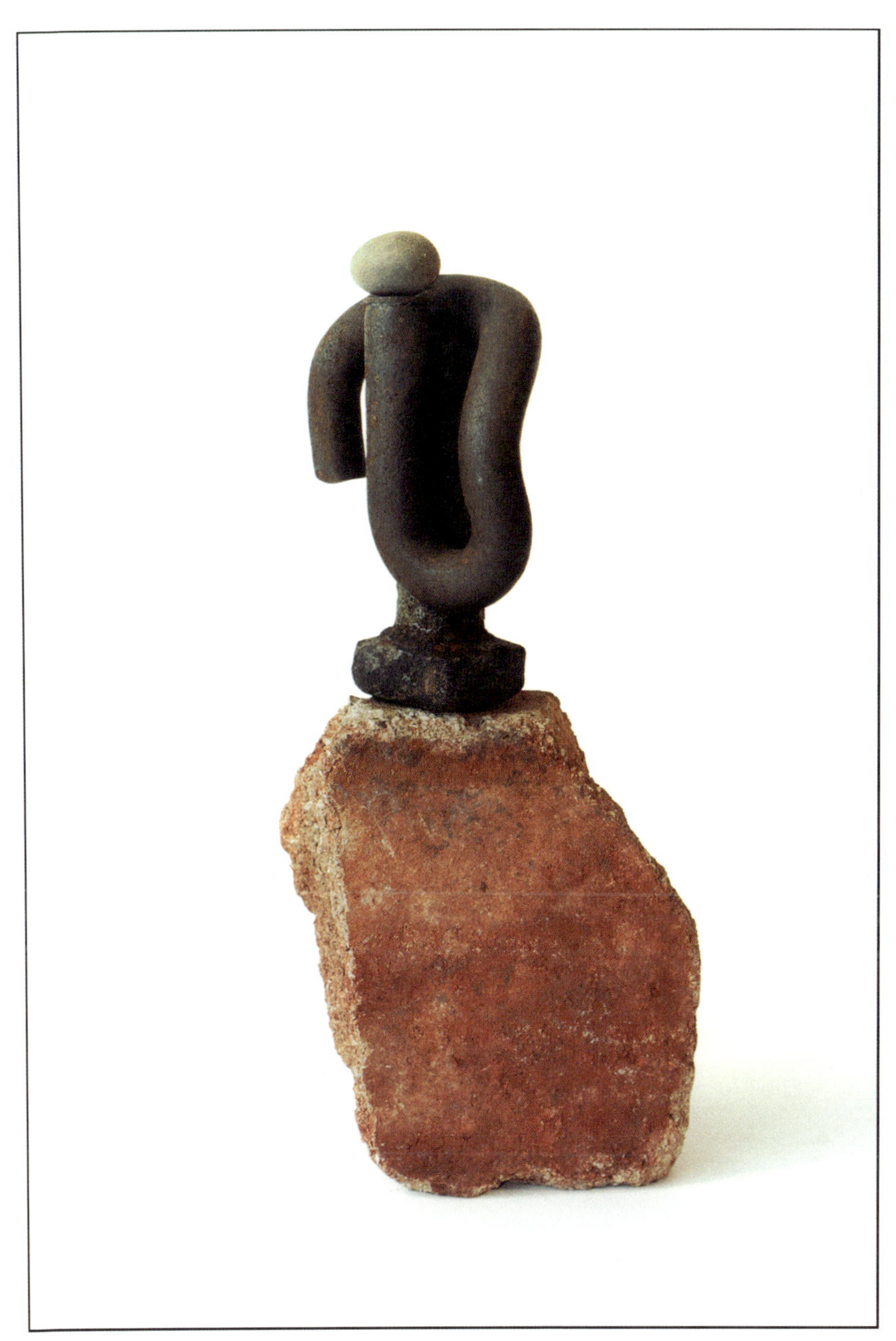

Stheno, 2005
Brick, rusting steel and stone, 12.75 x 6 x 5 inches

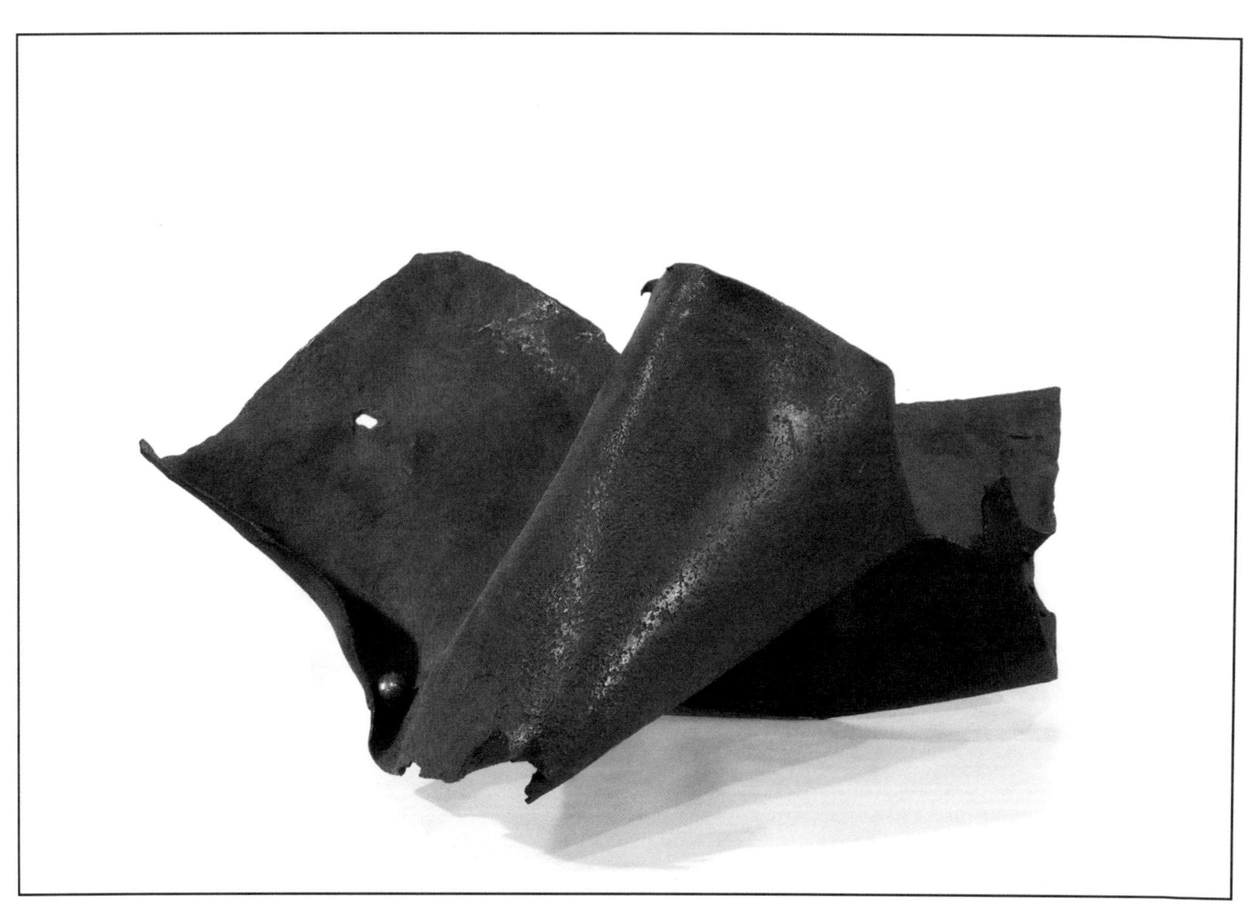

Thanatos, 2005
Rusting steel, 13.50 x 25.50 x 21 inches

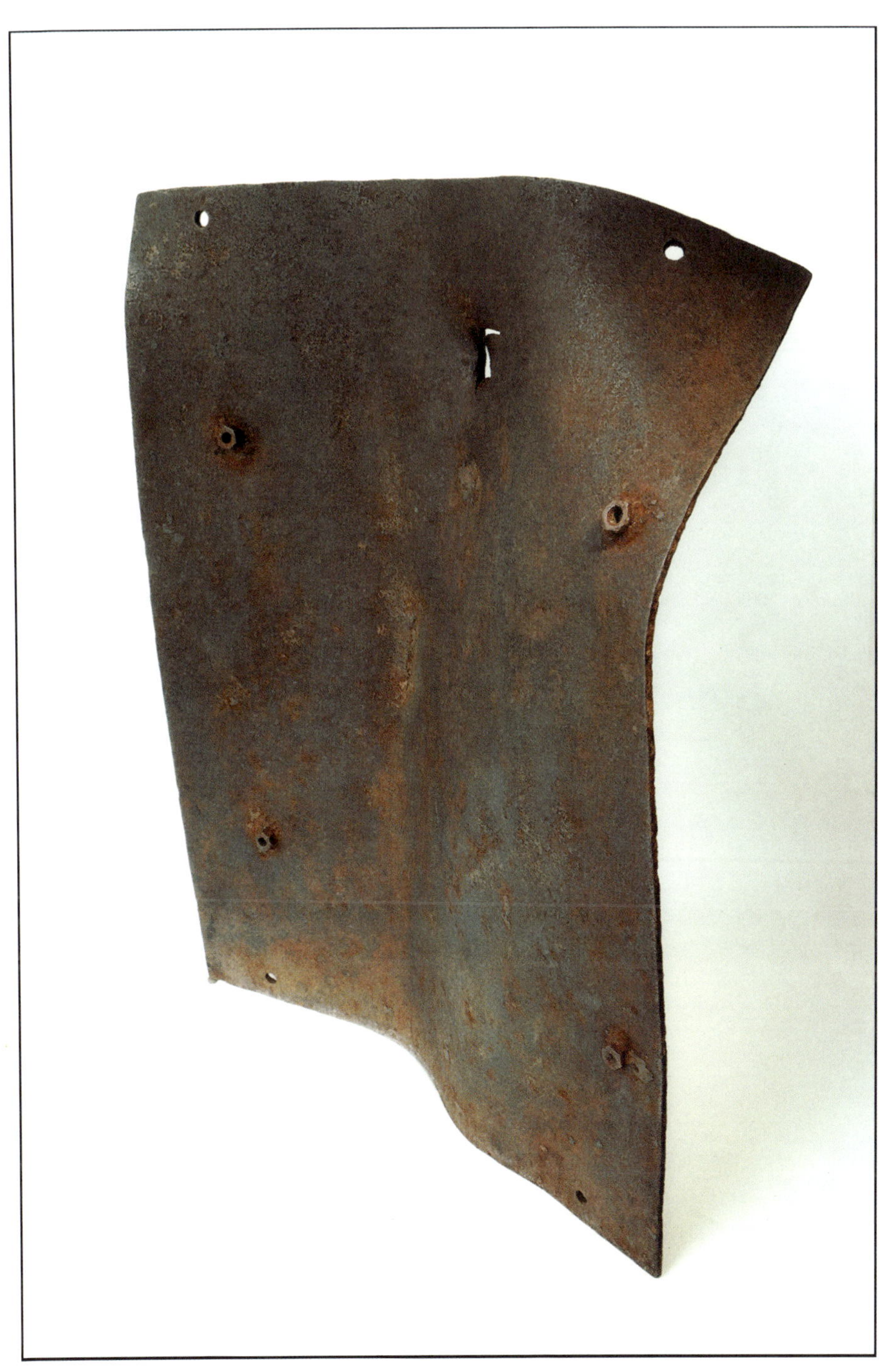

Fatum, 2005
Rusting steel and stone, 36.50 x 28 x 9 inches

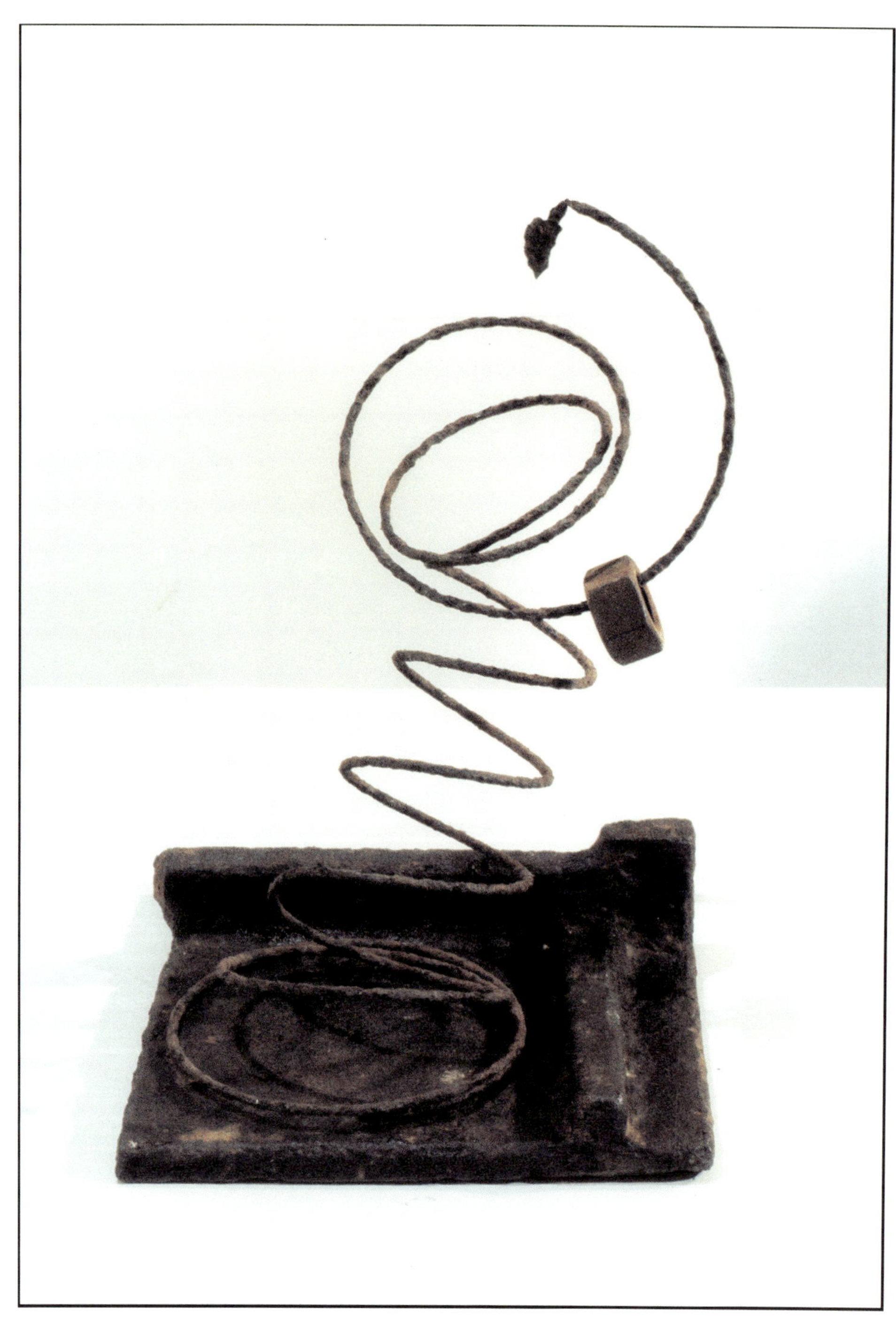

Euthenia, 2005
Rusting steel, 11.50 x 7.50 x 8 inches

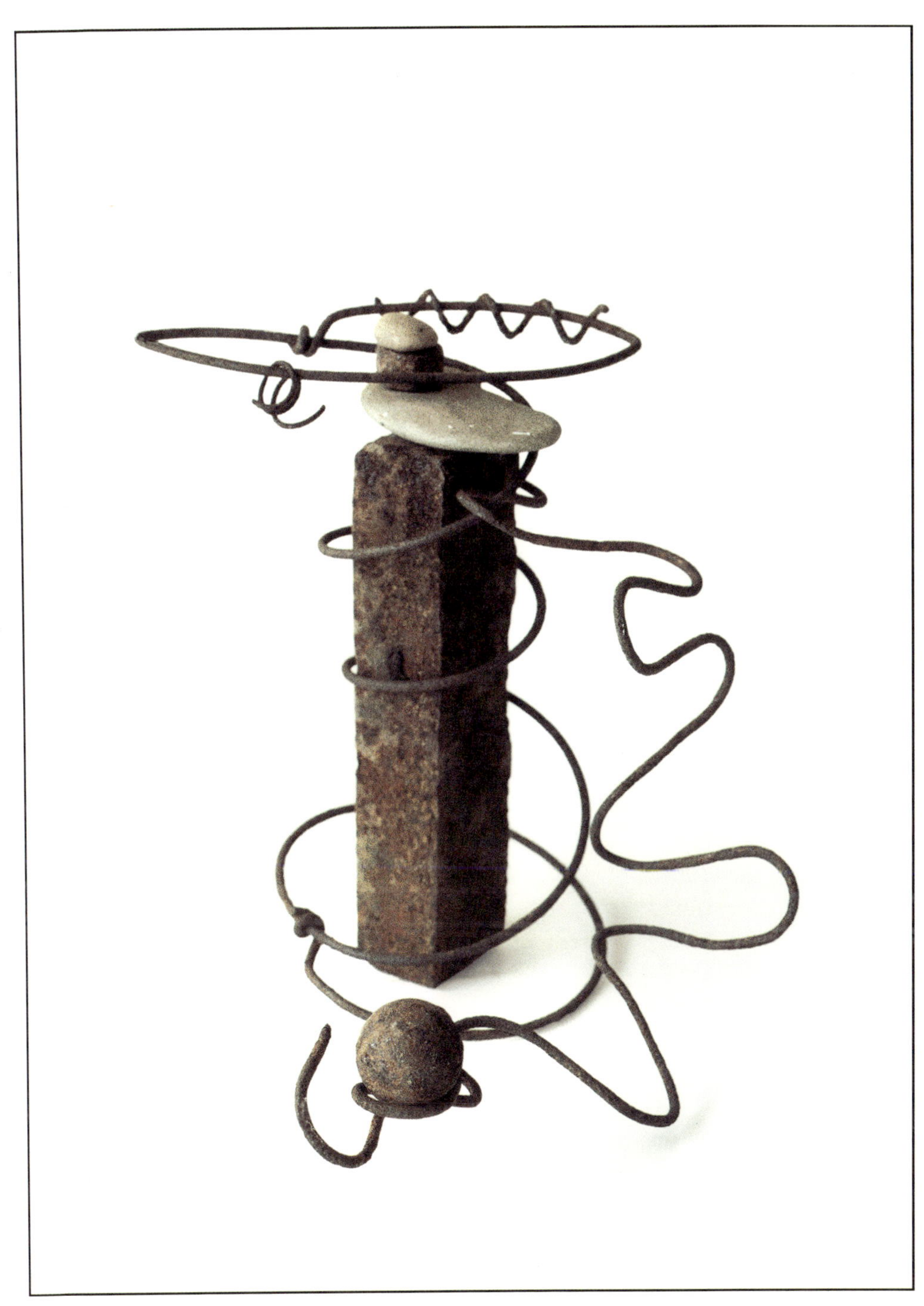

Psyche, 2005
Rusting steel, wire and stone, 6.25 x 9 x 7 inches

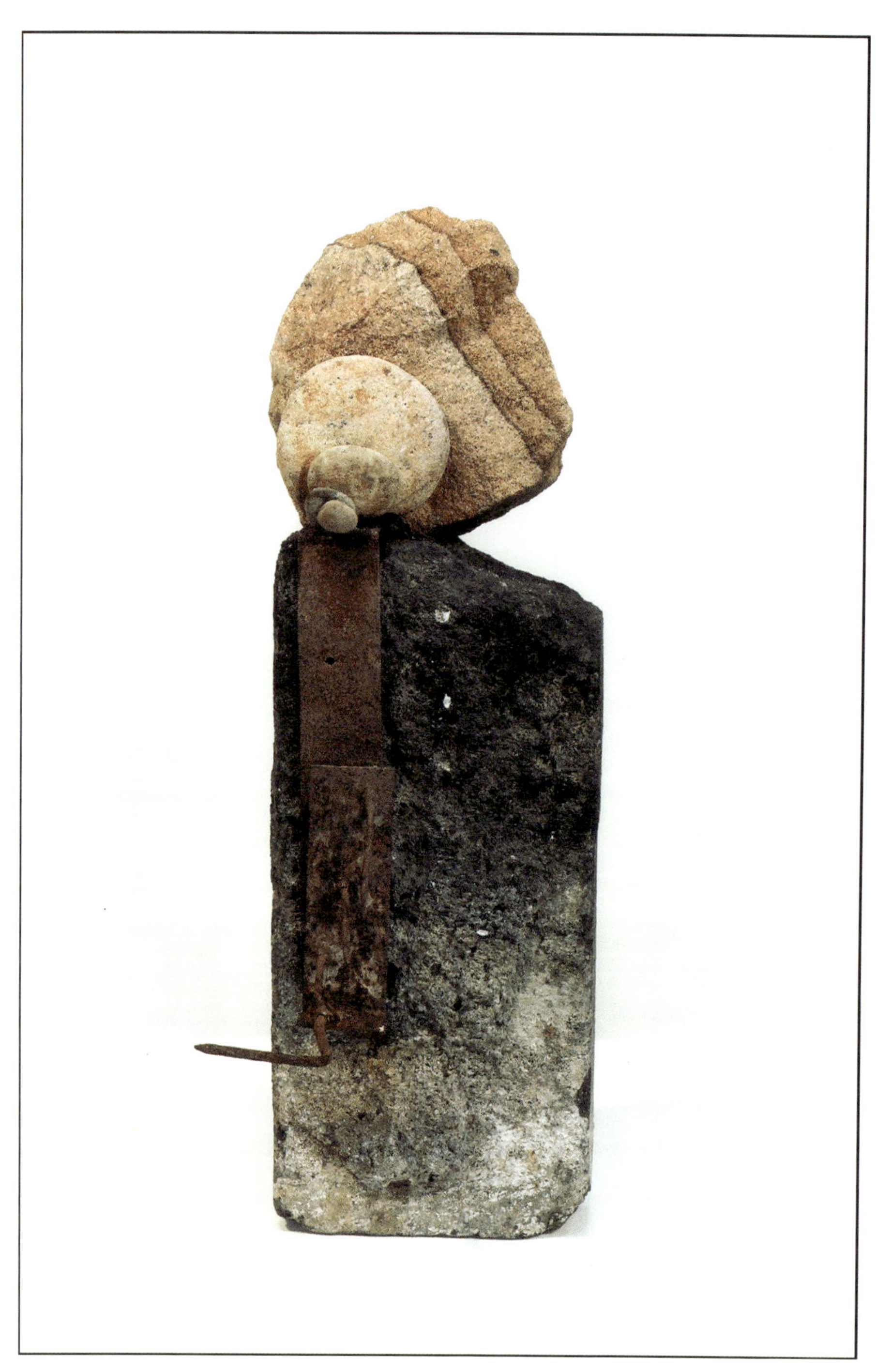

Proteus, 2003
Brick, rusting steel and stone, 12.25 x 4.50 x 5 inches

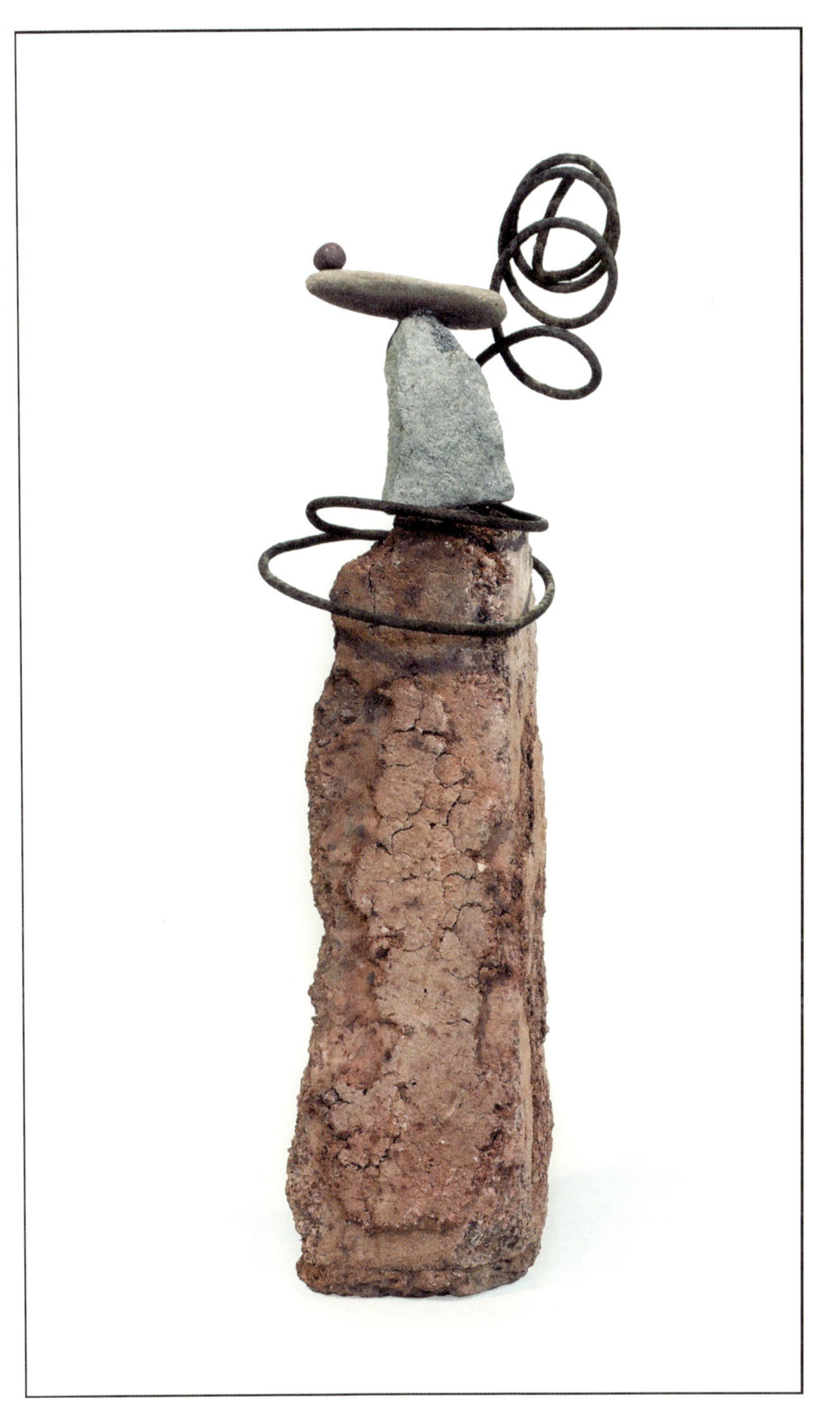

Cronos, 2003
Brick, rusting steel and stone, 13.50 x 6 x 5 inches

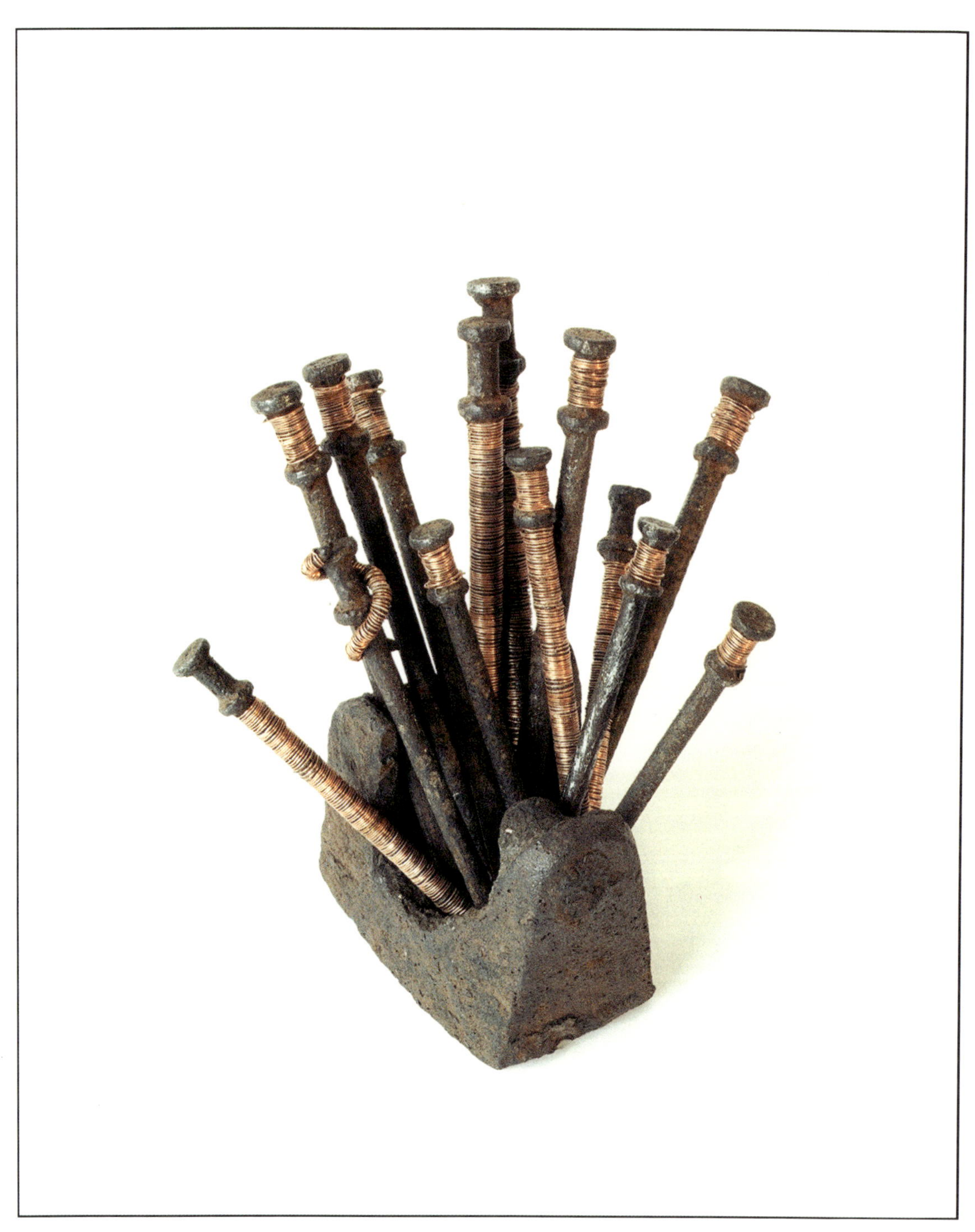

Naiads, 2005
Rusting steel and copper wire, 3.25 x 3.50 x 3.75 inches

A Note from August R. Carlino

President & Chief Executive Officer
Rivers of Steel National Heritage Area

When I was born, the steel mills had long established themselves as part of the Pittsburgh and southwestern Pennsylvania landscape. Like kids everywhere in the region, I went to sleep in the evening with the glow of an orange sky as a night light.

The mills were a shared experience for generations of Pittsburghers. They were big and black, a steady background to the hustle and bustle of daily life. It seemed as if everyone had a family member working in the mills. Businesses set their hours to coincide with shift turns at the mill. The rise of the steel industry attracted masses of workers from around the country and the world, fusing their cultural traditions with the already unique character of southwestern Pennsylvania.

Although steel production here is no longer in its heyday, the drama of the story remains– a story that reveals the birth and growth of an industry that changed the world. Occasionally, Rivers of Steel is presented with the opportunity to work with artists whose work enhances this story and our mission, like Michael Picarsic and Lorraine Vullo's *Recrudescence*. Salvaging broken, twisted pieces of a Jones & Laughlin steel mill from the site of its demolition, Michael and Lorraine created sculptures and photographs that distill remembrance, rebirth and a new purpose from these relics of a fallen mill.

Their work reminds me that Rivers of Steel and its partners face a similar task. A rich cultural and industrial history binds the region and its communities together. This is the vital resource Rivers of Steel and its heritage development partners draw upon to sculpt a creative future from the region's past.

Acknowledgments

When we started this project our only parameter was that we would not say "no" to any idea. We would pursue our ideas and see where they would lead us. We gratefully acknowledge all of you who also did not say no:

Thanks to the staff of Rivers of Steel National Heritage Area, Ron Baraff, Bostick & Sullivan, Robert D. Brevard, Pamela Z. Bryan, August R. Carlino, Carnegie Museum of Art, Jim Carver, Janis Dofner, Doris Dyen, Kristen Fair, Susan Golomb, Grubby, Dan Higgins, Gregory Holsinger, Murray Horne, Charlie Humphrey, Gerri Kay, Brian Kerr, J.B. Kreider Printing Company, Donald Kuspit, Brian Lang, Jeffrey T. Leber, Dennis Marsico, Ed Massery, Mon Valley Initiative, Angie Morini, Mary Navarro, Dave OBryan, Michael Paranzino, Mark Perrott, Jeanne Pearlman, Rose Marie Pera, Christine & Michael Picarsic, Jessica Picarsic, Jane Quinn, Lisa M. Rasmussen, Laura Robino, Linda Rose, Jen Saffron, Jean Salvato, Philip Salvato, Karen Scofield, Graham Shearing, Ian Short, Henry J. Simonds, Walt Sims, Loretta A. Stanish, Daniel Steinitz, Sukolsky-Brunelle Visual Media Lab, Judith Tener, Thomas Underiner, Antoinette L. Vullo, Frank V. Vullo, Simon Vullo Underiner, Deborah Witte, Wood Street Galleries and Michael Wurster. To the construction workers who helped unearth some of the treasures, the police officers that did not arrest us, the countless people whose smiles encouraged us. A very big shout out to Preston Allen. Thanks to all who kept us safe.

Michael Picarsic III and Lorraine Vullo

This project was funded in part by the generous support of the Fisher Fund and the A.W. Mellon Educational & Charitable Trust Fund of The Pittsburgh Foundation, with additional funding by the Henry John Simonds Foundation. Special thanks to the Steel Industry Heritage Corporation for their support.

The negatives from the Construction series have been printed into two portfolios: one as Van Dyke prints on watercolor paper; and one as sepia/selenium split-toned gelatin silver prints. Each portfolio consists of contact prints of the original 4" x 5", 5" x 7" and 11" x 14" negatives, printed in an edition of five.